Build a Great Team!

PEARSON EDUCATION LIMITED

Head Office:
Edinburgh Gate
Harlow CM20 2JE
Tel: +44 (0)1279 623623
Fax: +44 (0)1279 431059

London Office:
128 Long Acre, London WC2E 9AN
Tel: +44 (0)270 447 2000
Fax: +44 (0)270 240 5771
www.business-minds.com

First published in Great Britain in 1995

ISBN 0 273 64482 3

British Library Cataloguing in Publication Data
A CIP catalogue record for this book can be obtained from the British Library.

Typeset by Northern Phototypesetting Co. Ltd, Bolton
Printed and bound in Great Britain by Biddles Ltd, Guildford and King's Lynn

The Publishers' policy is to use paper manufactured from sustainable forests.

Contents

Acknowledgements

I would like to thank Dr Meredith Belbin for his help with the section of this book pertaining to his work on team roles. For anyone interested in reading further on the subject I can highly recommend Dr Belbin's books *Management Teams: Why They Succeed or Fail* and *Team Roles At Work*, both published by Butterworth-Heinemann.

Of the best rulers,
The people only know that they exist;
The next best they love and praise;
The next they fear;
And the next they revile.
When they do not command the people's faith,
Some will lose faith in them,
And then they resort to oaths!
But of the best when their task is accomplished, their work done,
The people all remark, 'we have done it ourselves'.

Lao-Tzu (6th Century B.C.)

Introduction

Have you ever wished you were organised, full of ideas, a great diplomat, a natural leader, a brilliant analyst, a thorough researcher and an extrovert sales person, with an eye for detail and an instinct for seeing the whole problem? It's a bit of a tall order, really. In fact, several of those qualities are mutually exclusive. That's why working in teams is so valuable. As long as we can muster all these qualities between us, there's no need for every single member of the team to have every useful ability or skill.

The first skill successful managers need is to be able to select the best people to work with them. Your job will be vastly easier if you have built up a group of people around you whose skills and natural abilities complement each other. The first chapter in this book is about how to do precisely that.

Once you have assembled your working group, you need to turn it into a team. It's difficult to define exactly what the difference is between a team and a group of people paid to work in the same department or on the same project – the answer is very complex – but essentially it has to do with attitude. The people involved have to be made to feel a strong identity with the group in order for it to become a team. And that's your job.

Perhaps the most vital managerial function of all is to be able to generate that elusive ingredient: team spirit. And the skills you need in order to do this are all 'people' skills. The bulk of this book examines those skills, and identifies not only the best way to handle particular people or situations, but also the reasons why these techniques work.

Is it worth it? There are an awful lot of skills to master, and some of them call for a good deal of work: planning, thinking, preparing. Why not just settle for managing a group of people who happen to work in the same department? Does it really make much difference, this team spirit stuff? Well yes, it does. Here are just a few of the benefits of working as a team:

- it improves morale and motivation
- it reduces staff turnover
- productivity increases
- job satisfaction is improved
- it's far easier to overcome problems when everyone is working together.

Don't forget that you're not outside the team, organising and running it. You're a part of it, leading from within. So you gain all these benefits too – you'll be better motivated, have higher job satisfaction and so on, and any increase in productivity that reflects well on the team, will also reflect well on you as team leader.

It's not really as hard as it might seem. Once you grasp the underlying principles of dealing with people effectively and positively, you'll find you instinctively start to build those principles into your natural response whenever you're faced with a difficult situation or a person who needs careful handling.

The three piece jigsaw

As a manager, there are three aspects of a team that you need to develop in order to create a great team. The leadership expert John Adair uses a Venn diagram to illustrate this.

As you can see, the three things you have to consider are the task, the group and the individual. Each impinges on the other two, and to ignore any one of them considerably reduces the effectiveness of the other two.

If you focus only on the group and the individuals in it, you have a great working environment but nothing actually gets done. If you just concentrate on the task and the individuals working on it, you lose sight of the group and people will start to pull in different directions. If you ignore the individuals, the job may get done efficiently but morale starts to wane as people lose sight of their personal value and contribution.

This is part of the answer to the question of what defines a team as opposed to a group of people who work together. The members of a team share a common goal, and

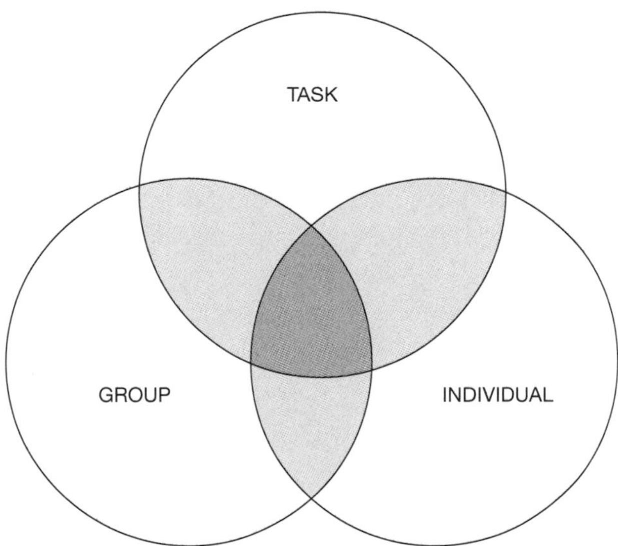

this goal lies at the point where the three circles overlap. They share the same ambitions for the success of the team in terms of the projects and tasks it undertakes, in terms of the group as a whole, and in terms of developing the individuals within it.

Leader or servant?

In order to achieve this triple focus in your team, try thinking of your own role not so much as team leader but as team servant. Your job is to keep the team together and motivated, while their job is to get the task done. And you keep the team together by working on their behalf, not by telling them what to do. For example, you need to ask them what equipment, information and resources they need in order to do the job properly. Then you can negotiate on their behalf with other managers and departments to give them what they need.

This point is perfectly illustrated by Herman Hesse's *Journey to the East*. A group of men on a journey decide they need a servant to do their cooking, cleaning and other menial tasks while they are travelling. They visit a monastery and ask if anyone can be spared to serve them on their journey. The monks offer them one of their order, Leo, but explains that he can only travel with them for a certain distance and then he will have to leave them and return.

Leo looks after them and does their chores and keeps their spirits up, and all goes well until Leo leaves them at the prearranged point on their journey. Gradually, the party's morale flags and the group falls apart. Eventually, their journey is abandoned. One of the men wanders for several years and finally finds himself back at the monastery that Leo came from. When he enters he discovers that far from being a humble servant, Leo is in fact the great and revered head of the order of monks.

This story should illustrate the importance of being a servant to your team. Many managers feel their job is to 'give the orders', and fear that they will lose respect if they are seen to step out of this role. However, once you are leading a team, and not simply a group of people, you will be judged – by the team members and those outside – by the performance of the whole team. Since adopting the role of team servant will improve that performance, it therefore follows that it will reflect well on you and your team.

Before we start …

There is one thing above all that it is essential to understand about people before you can manage them as members of a successful team, and it is this: *you cannot change people's personalities*. As soon as you try to do that, you are doomed to fail. You can encourage them to adapt their behaviour; that's a different thing. Let's take an example from outside the working environment.

When you're at home, are you a tidy person or an untidy one? Most couples who live together differ in this to some extent, and it's a frequent cause of arguments. One thinks the other is trying to make them live in a pigsty, and the other thinks their partner is creating unnecessary stress, and if they'd just relax they'd see it wasn't that important. So the tidy one tries to turn their partner into a tidy person, which creates resentment. Meanwhile the other tries to make their tidy partner into a more laid back kind of person who isn't really bothered about whether the towels live on the towel rail or on the bathroom floor. The tidy partner is angry at this attempt to change them.

The fact is, we can't change. If we could, we would do it and save the arguments. But because we *think* we can change the other person, we're upset and annoyed when they don't change. Our expectations of creating the kind of person we want aren't being met.

How about a different approach? Suppose we accept that we can't change the other person, so we stop trying. However, we can encourage them to adapt their behaviour. So if you're the tidy one, try saying: 'I know you're not a tidy person. Could you, sometimes, be a messy person who puts the towels back on the rail?' It helps to be specific about your requests, and to limit them to a maximum of two or three at a time. This has two effects:

1. **You have lowered your expectations, and no longer expect 100 per cent tidiness from them, so you'll be happier to settle for only 75 per cent.**
2. **They feel you're accepting them for what they are, so they have no need to feel angry or resentful.**

This usually leads to all sorts of other solutions because you can now have a friendly discussion where you both accept the other one's standpoint. It often leads, for example, to divvying up tasks differently. It's not that big a deal to hang up their towels for them on the odd occasions they forget, and in exchange, they can do a couple of the jobs you really hate, like cleaning the old bits of hair out of the basin U-bend when the plughole won't drain.

Back to work. Perhaps someone on your team is prone to forget or miss out minor tasks. It might be because they're the kind of person who thinks in terms of whole projects and sees the bigger picture clearly – perhaps they're the one who always spots the flaw in the overall plan in time to do something about it. So they're a useful person to have on the team, but they are forgetful about the little things. Don't try to turn them into someone who doesn't make minor mistakes. You'll demoralise them and depress yourself when it doesn't work. By all means tackle the subject, but don't expect them to change their personality. Simply ask them to be someone who sees the broad sweep of a project, and does their best to keep on top of the minor details as well.

Much of the art of managing people involves identifying people's natural strengths and weaknesses. Once you've done that, you can find ways to capitalise on their strengths. When it comes to the weaknesses, you need to work out what causes them – is it lack of interest, lack of skill, or a personality whose natural talents simply don't lie in that direction? Where the weakness is due to the person's innate personality, it's better to work around it – perhaps even giving some tasks to another member of the team – than to try to force the person to confront and overcome it.

If you have an enthusiastic and motivated team working with you, most people problems are a result of trying to squeeze square pegs into round holes. Once you have taken on board the principle that you can't change people's personalities, you can eliminate just about all of these problems. This book is about how to apply this principle to different types of people and in different situations.

So, you've picked a group of people with the right combination of skills and personalities. You've found a way to develop their strengths and eliminate or avoid their weaknesses. You've inspired them: they're positive, motivated and share a group identity – they're a team. And now they can get on with the project, or the work of the department, on their own. You've done it. You've built a great team.

So now what are you going to do? Well, you can't afford to sit back and relax for long: your team's morale will start to wane, good people will look around for other, more stimulating jobs and the team will slowly begin pulling in different directions again. The final chapter of this book is all about the techniques you need to adopt in order to maintain team spirit, improve your team's performance, develop the individuals within it, and build an even greater team!

CHAPTER ONE

Team functions

We're all different. But it's surprising how many qualities we expect everybody to share when they're at work. I'm not talking about skills, which we can all learn, but styles of working and strengths and weaknesses which are a part of our personalities. We tend to expect everyone to generate ideas when they're needed, or to be diplomatic in dealing with other departments and organisations, or to be thorough in dealing with the small but important details of the tasks we ask them to perform.

When you think about it, this is ludicrous of course. Certainly there are skills we can learn which will improve our performance in these areas to some extent, but essentially our qualities are part of our make up and we will always be better at some things than others. However the good news is that if we work in teams, it doesn't really matter – not on an individual level. What matters is that the team as a whole has access to these talents. You need someone on your team who can generate new ideas, but you don't need everyone to be able to do it. In fact, that could lead to a great deal of conflict and create more problems than solutions.

A team leader needs to assemble a group of individuals who between them add up to a whole – the team – which is greater than the sum of its parts. To do this, you need to identify the individual personality types to include in your team to make sure that every useful quality is included somewhere. Well, you're in luck, because it's already been done for you. Dr Meredith Belbin has spent over twenty years researching the nature, structure and behaviour of teams, and his highly respected work on Team

Role Theory provides a clear profile of the basic personality types you need to include in an effective team. Dr Belbin has identified nine team roles, which we will examine in this chapter. In addition, this chapter will look at:

- **what happens if the mix on the team is not right;**
- **how to fit nine personality types into a team with only two or three members;**
- **how to correct an unbalanced team.**

Functional roles and team roles

Dr Belbin highlights the distinction between functional roles and team roles. Functional roles are the ones we all know about: the tasks listed in the job description. When we interview prospective team members we tend to focus on the functional role, and we select them on the basis of their skills, abilities and experience in that area – telesales, personnel, quality management, finance, marketing, production or whatever.

The team role, however, is equally important. It is the role we adopt in terms of our contribution and relationships with the rest of the team whenever we work as part of a collective. It is determined by our inherent personality, and learned behaviour, rather than by our skills, experience or technical knowledge. Are we slapdash or finicky by nature, for example? For this reason, each of us is likely to adopt roughly the same team role in every team we work in, from the board of directors to the committee of the local residents' association. It may adapt slightly according to the personalities of the other team members, but in essence it won't vary very much.

The first step in building a great team is to bring together the right people to form it. If you recognise the nine team roles described by Dr Belbin, and can match your team members to them, you have the foundation for a hugely successful team. It will be able to achieve far more than the combined efforts of all its members working independently would, however talented they are.

Furthermore, if everyone has a role that suits them as a person, as well as suiting their skills, they will feel they are making a greater contribution. They will receive more recognition and appreciation. There will be fewer confrontations and clashes within the team because people will value their own unique contribution and not compete for roles with other team members. In fact, these are all factors which contribute to greater motivation and stronger morale. In other words, once you have constructed a strong team in which everyone has a role, you have made the rest of your job far easier for yourself.

The nine team roles

There follows below a rundown of the nine key roles that Dr Belbin has identified, using the names that he has evolved over the years. If people possess the characteristics of their team type very strongly, there are certain less desirable qualities that are virtually bound to go along with these. For example, if you are a perfectionist you probably have a tendency to spend too much time on minor details. Each of these team roles has both positive qualities and what Dr Belbin terms 'allowable weaknesses'; the price you should expect, and be prepared, to pay for the positive qualities. After each of the nine roles you'll find a brief guide to differentiating between that role and any others that it can easily be confused with.

Plant

These people are highly intelligent, original thinkers; their great skill is in generating new ideas and solving difficult problems. They scatter the seeds which the rest of the team nourish until they bear fruit. The Plant is the ideas person. That is not to say that other members of the team don't have ideas too, but the Plant thinks in a radical, imaginitive and lateral way. However, Plants are not the best people to put their own ideas into practice – they lose interest quickly and since they are more concerned with major issues than minor details they tend to miss out on details and make careless mistakes.

Plants usually prefer to work fairly independently; they are individualistic and often unconventional. They are usually introverted, and can be prickly to work with. They are sensitive to criticism and praise, but often dismissive of other people's ideas, and don't easily communicate on a wavelength other than their own; they expect other people to adjust to them.

Plants can be inclined to devote too much time to ideas which spark their imagination but don't match the team's needs or objectives. If you put too many Plants together it can be surprisingly unproductive – they can each become entrenched and competitive with ideas, and simply fight their own corner without being prepared to take on each other's proposals.

SUMMARY

Individualistic, serious-minded, unorthodox.

Positive qualities: genius, imagination, intellect, knowledge. Solves difficult problems.

Allowable weaknesses: up in the clouds, inclined to disregard practical details or protocol.

Resource Investigator

Resource Investigators are also creative, but they don't generate new ideas in the way that Plants do. They are more likely to take a raw idea from someone else and develop it. They are relaxed, extrovert and inquisitive, and usually extremely popular. They are skilled diplomats and negotiators, and can think on their feet. Their positive and optimistic nature can be a valuable influence on the team's morale and motivation.

The Resource Investigator looks outward, and has plenty of contacts outside the team. Quick to recognise new opportunities, they will either be out of the office or on the phone finding out what is available and negotiating the best deals. Throughout all this they will be firing the rest of the team with enthusiasm. And this is where their greatest value lies: they preserve the team from stagnation and inertia.

Resource Investigators rely heavily on stimulation from other people – although they often initiate the enthusiasm, it flags very quickly if they don't get positive feedback from the rest of the team. They are also prone to lose interest once a project gets underway, and can fail to follow up tasks.

SUMMARY

Extrovert, enthusiastic, curious, communicative.

Positive qualities: a capacity for contacting useful people and exploring new opportunities. An ability to respond to challenges.

Allowable weaknesses: liable to lose interest once the initial fascination has passed. Can be over-optimistic and uncritical.

Plants and Resource Investigators are the two most creative team roles. However, they are easy to tell apart:

- Plants generate original ideas whereas Resource Investigators tend to build creatively on other people's ideas;
- Plants prefer to work alone while Resource Investigators need the stimulus of others;
- Plants work better in a liberal and loosely structured environment; Resource Investigators operate well under pressure and cope well in a crisis;
- Plants are serious-minded and are often loners, while Resource Investigators are relaxed and gregarious.

Example: imagine your team has been discussing customer complaints. A number of customers have been unhappy with what they see as an overcomplicated procedure for getting repairs done, which involves them having to deal with three different departments. You want to find a different way of resolving these problems so that the customer only needs to deal with one contact in your organisation. The Plant's likely response is 'Give me a little while to think about it and I'll come up with a solution.' The Resource Investigator, on the other hand, will say 'I'll have a chat with the other two departments and we'll find a way to do it.'

Co-ordinator

The Co-ordinator is highly disciplined and controlled, and has a natural inclination to focus on objectives. This helps to keep the team as a whole working towards a shared goal. The Co-ordinator is the great unifying force within the team, and is usually highly respected by the other members of it.

Co-ordinators are confident and usually have a natural air of authority; they are good delegators, good communicators and are adept at spotting individual talent and harnessing it for the benefit of the whole team. For this reason, they are often the ones who establish the roles and work boundaries of the others, and not surprisingly they often become team leaders. However they can be valuable in a team without necessarily being the leader.

Co-ordinators are wise and emotionally mature; they are not significantly more intelligent than the rest of the group, nor are they highly creative. Their strength lies in their ability to extract these skills from others, and direct them towards the team's overall objectives. They can pull together a team with diverse skills and personalities, and can sum up group feeling and articulate the team's collective view.

SUMMARY

Calm, self-confident, controlled.

Positive qualities: a capacity for treating and welcoming all potential contributors on their merits and without prejudice. A clear sense of objectives.

Allowable weaknesses: not of exceptional intellect or creative ability.

Resource Investigators and Co-ordinators are both good at liaising with others and motivating the team. However they do this in quite distinct ways:

- Resource Investigators enjoy challenge and excitement and revel in making new contacts and locating resources, while Co-ordinators prefer to take the resources available and direct them towards the team or organisation's objectives;
- Resource Investigators tend to look outwards at useful resources and contacts outside the team, whereas Co-ordinators are focused more inwardly on the team itself.

Example: the team is discussing the promotion of an important and exciting new product. An idea is mooted that instead of simply running an advertising campaign as usual, it might be worthwhile holding a series of unusual or quirky special events to draw attention to the new product. The Resource Investigator is already half way out of the room, saying 'Leave it with me; I'll check out the possibilities and get back to you.' The Co-ordinator, meanwhile, is still sitting at the meeting table asking 'Has anyone got anything else to suggest before we start work on this?'

Shaper

These personality types are dynamic and full of nervous energy. They are outgoing, impulsive and impatient, and often edgy – sometimes verging on paranoid. They love to set challenges and to be challenged, and they are very achievement orientated. They want results, and will push others to achieve them; this can lead to rows, but these may not last long and grudges will be quickly forgotten.

The Shaper's chief function is to help shape the team's efforts. Shapers are always looking for a pattern in discussions, and trying to unite ideas, objectives and practical considerations into a single feasible project which they will then promote urgently for decision and action.

The Shaper's compulsive drive makes things happen, and for this reason they are often natural team leaders. They appear highly confident, even though they are often full of self-doubt and only reassured by results. They work well in politically-charged situations because they tend to rise above the problems and carry on regardless, and they don't mind confrontation or taking unpopular decisions.

SUMMARY

Highly strung, outgoing, dynamic.

Positive qualities: drive and a readiness to challenge inertia, ineffectiveness, complacency or self-deception.

Allowable weaknesses: prone to provocation, irritation and impatience. A tendency to hurt people's feelings.

Co-ordinators and Shapers are both strong leaders, but with very different styles:

- Co-ordinators tend to be 'social' leaders, whereas Shapers function more as 'task' leaders;
- Co-ordinators look for the best in people and exploit these talents fully, while Shapers expect to be followed;
- Co-ordinators are calm and relaxed; Shapers are dynamic and thrive on nervous energy;
- Co-ordinators see themselves as part of the team, while Shapers tend to see the team as an extension of themselves;
- Co-ordinators and Shapers have such different management styles that they are prone to clash if they work together at the same status level;
- Shapers often need to work under a Co-ordinator: they need recognition more, and the Co-ordinator provides them with it.

Example: a very large order has just come in which is also urgent. In order to fulfil it – along with all the other orders that are due – the next fortnight's production schedule will have to be completely reworked. The production team spends over an hour going through all the details and reorganising the schedule. When they get to the end, the Co-ordinator suggests spending another five minutes going through the whole thing once, to make sure that everyone is clear about the changes. The Shaper is champing at the bit, saying 'We haven't got time for all that. Let's just get on and do it – we can sort out any problems along the way.'

Monitor Evaluator

These people are intelligent, stable and introverted. They can be rather dry and unexciting personalities – even cold. Their strength lies not in generating ideas but in clear, dispassionate analysis of other people's ideas. They weigh up all the pros and cons, are shrewd judges and seldom make bad decisions. It is most often the Monitor Evaluator who prevents the team from committing itself to a misguided course of action.

Monitor Evaluators are objective thinkers, and take their time to reach conclusions. They don't tend to criticise for the sake of it but because they can see a flaw in the plan or the argument. They are fairly unemotional and unenthusiastic, often quite hard to motivate, but this has the advantage that their judgements are highly objective and rarely clouded by personal or egotistical considerations. They can be tactless and even damaging to team morale because they tend to express their views bluntly, but they are always fair and balanced.

It is important to keep Monitor Evaluators well motivated and positive or they can become a negative influence within the team. But give them large quantities of written material and other data requiring complex analysis, and they will do the job better than anyone. Ask them to analyse problems, draw up plans or assess other people's contributions, and they will come up trumps every time.

SUMMARY

Sober, unemotional, prudent.

Positive qualities: judgement, discretion, hard-headedness.

Allowable weaknesses: lack of enthusiasm or the ability to motivate other people – can be uninspired and uninspiring; a bit of a cold fish.

Plants and Monitor Evaluators are both intelligent thinkers, but they think very differently from each other:

- Plants generate new ideas whereas Monitor Evaluators process other people's ideas;
- Plants operate through inspiration and intuition; Monitor Evaluators think in a thorough, analytical way. They never make snap judgements;
- Plants will sometimes offer undeveloped ideas for the team to build on together, whereas Monitor Evaluators will reserve comment until they have thought through the issue fully, and will then deliver a complete assessment;
- Plants are keen to promote their own ideas, while Monitor Evaluators are introvert and have no emotional investment in having their views accepted.

Example: you've been going through a thick file which contains the results of a survey you commissioned to find out which faults are most commonly reported on your products. It seems that the hinge on the door frequently fails, but the design team say this is unavoidable because of the unequal stress you will always get on a side hinge. You have a chat with the Plant on your team, who says 'I've got it! How about a double hinge on the door to balance the stress? Or perhaps we could even put the door on the top instead of at the front.' Next you go and speak to the Monitor Evaluator, and explain the problem to them. Their response is 'If you give me the file I'll go through it and then let you know what I think.' You mention the Plant's suggestions and the Monitor Evaluator replies 'That may be a possibility. I'll keep it in mind while I go through the file.'

Team Worker

The Team Worker is supportive, sensitive and social, and recognises the emotional undercurrents in the team most clearly. These people make good listeners and diplomats, loyal to the team, popular and mild natured. Their instinctive reaction to new ideas is to build on them rather than pick holes in them.

The presence of the Team Worker minimises interpersonal problems in the team, and they are particularly valuable in teams whose members are prone to conflict. Not surprisingly they are relatively uncompetitive, and can be indecisive at times, but they are hugely important to morale, especially at times of stress or crisis.

As leaders, Team Workers are popular, unthreatening and very motivating, although they can lack dynamism.

SUMMARY

Socially orientated, rather mild, sensitive.

Positive qualities: ability to respond to people and situations and promote team spirit. A good diplomat.

Allowable weaknesses: indecisive in moments of crisis; they are adapters rather than changers.

Co-ordinators and Team Workers act to promote harmony and team spirit using different styles:

- Co-ordinators point everyone towards the same direction, whereas Team Workers identify areas of friction between individuals and smooth out one-to-one relationships;
- Co-ordinators provide a clear objective for the team. Team Workers like to contribute to setting the objective; they are very comfortable once the objective is clear;
- Co-ordinators are good at dealing with difficult people from the position of leader, while Team Workers often work well under difficult people.

Example: an important decision needs to be made and there's disagreement in the team on which is the best course to take. It becomes clear that no one is going to change their view and a unanimous decision is impossible. The Co-ordinator calls the team together and explains that there is no point discussing it forever with no clear conclusion. 'Opinion is fairly equally divided, but a decision needs to be made. Since the first option is the one that most clearly fits our objectives, that is the route we shall take.' In the same situation, the Team Worker leader talks to each member of the team individually, asking not only what their view is but also how they will feel if the other option is taken. Once the Team Worker has determined which is the best decision, they speak individually to those who disagreed with it to try and encourage them to support it.

Implementer

So far our team is full of people who can generate and analyse ideas, give direction to the group, lead the other team members, and keep morale going – but who's going to do the core work of the team? The Implementer. This is the person who has the organisational skills, common sense and self-discipline to turn ideas and decisions into defined and manageable tasks. Implementers convert general plans into plans of action. They are hard-working and systematic, as well as being loyal and without any strong self-interest. One of the Implementer's greatest assets is that they are happy to do any task that needs to be done, regardless of whether they personally enjoy doing it or not.

Implementers like to create order, and are uncomfortable in the face of sudden change. They are at their best drawing up schedules and budgets and charts, and setting up systems, and although they can be a little inflexible and prone to resist ideas they see as irrelevant, they are co-operative about adapting and fine-tuning their proposals.

SUMMARY

Conservative, dutiful, predictable.

Positive qualities: organising ability, practical common sense, hard-working, self-discipline.

Allowable weaknesses: lack of flexibility, slow to respond to new ideas, resistant to change.

Completer

Completers are anxious and introvert by nature, although they may come across as calm. They worry about what might go wrong so they are not happy until they have thoroughly checked every detail. As a result they are painstakingly conscientious – they make excellent proofreaders. Although Completers are not particularly assertive, they transmit a sense of urgency which permeates the whole team, and are intolerant of carelessness in others.

Because Completers are so orderly and thorough they find it hard to delegate, but they almost never fail to meet the high standards they set themselves, and they never **miss a deadline.**

SUMMARY

Painstaking, orderly, conscientious, anxious.

Positive qualities: a capacity to deliver what they promise, perfectionism.

Allowable weaknesses: inclined to worry unduly, reluctant to delegate, can be a nit-picker.

Implementers and Completers are the doers on the team:

- Implementers focus on systems, schedules and practical plans, whereas Completers concentrate on completing tasks thoroughly and in detail;
- Implementers are interested in finding the best method for getting the job done, while Completers are less concerned with the method than with the results.

Example: the team is responsible for organising a stand at a major trade show. All the key decisions have been made in terms of which products and services to focus on, what type of stand design to go for and which key customers and prospects to target with invitations. Now it's time to get down to the nitty gritty of planning and organising the details. The Implementer wants the team to agree exactly what schedules and plans they want drawn up, and is recommending that every single task, however small, should be allocated at the start so everyone is clear what's going on. The Completer is saying 'Once you've agreed the schedules pass them on to me so I can check at every stage that we're on schedule. And please make sure that every single stage has a clear deadline marked to get it done by.'

Specialist

Specialists are dedicated to acquiring highly specialised skills or knowledge. Their real interest is in their own subject area, which they advance enthusiastically and about which they adopt a highly professional attitude. However they tend to show little interest in anyone else's work and, indeed, they can be loners who show little interest in other people. Specialists possess the drive, dedication and single-mindedness to become thoroughgoing experts in a narrow field.

In teams whose activities are based on specialised skills or knowledge, the Specialist is a key player, and in these situations Specialists can make good managers because of their wealth of knowledge and concomitant ability to take decisions based on an in-depth understanding of the subject.

SUMMARY

Single-minded, self-starting, dedicated.

Positive qualities: provides knowledge and skills in rare supply.

Allowable weaknesses: contributes only on a narrow front. Tends not to see the big picture.

Completers and Specialists are both dedicated to achieving an extremely high standard, but from a different viewpoint:

- Completers aim for a high standard in anything they are asked to do; Specialists are interested only in their own field;
- Completers are happy to work for most types of manager, and they don't object to having their work overseen by someone else. Specialists dislike close supervision by anyone who knows less about their chosen field than they do.

Example: there's a project underway and you're worried that it might not be progressing as well as you hope. You talk to each member of the team about how their part of the work is going. When you come to the Completer, and ask how everything's going and whether they need any extra help, the response is 'It's fine – I've completed the first two stages and I'm halfway through the third. I'll certainly have it done by the date we agreed. Do you want to have a look at the work I've done so far?' Later on you have a word with the Specialist: 'How's it going? Do you need any extra help?' The Specialist's reply is 'I'm doing fine. No, I don't need any help thanks – I'll get it done much quicker if I'm left alone.'

How do you know which roles you and your team members fit into? Dr Belbin and his company Belbin Associates have put together a battery of tests over the last twenty years or so, including psychometric tests, self-assessment and assessment by colleagues. These are also available as a computer package (see the end of this chapter for details).

Finding the right mix

Of course, it's unlikely that you work in a team of nine people containing one perfect example of each type. In fact a few people don't really fall into any useful team role, and many others show characteristics of two or three types. It's useful to identify your team members' roles. Most will have at least one secondary role which they can comfortably take. Suppose you have two Plants and no Co-ordinator; you will probably find the Plants are frequently clashing with each other. But one of them may also be a Co-ordinator; ask them to chair the team and you've immediately created a far better mix, eliminating the conflict and providing the team with a Co-ordinator.

You will tend to find that if you have too many of one type on a team you will run into difficulties. Too many Shapers for instance (which may be as few as two) can lead to conflict and aggravation. But too many of the more diplomatic and laid back Team Workers and Implementers, for example, can result in a happy but low achieving team whose members place more emphasis on reaching agreement than on getting results.

Dr Belbin lists six key factors that most strongly influence the successfulness of the team:

1. **The person in the chair**. There needs to be someone fairly senior on the team (it doesn't have to be the team leader) whose profile closely matches that of the Co-ordinator and who can chair crucial discussions.

2. **One strong Plant in the team**. Successful teams need a good Plant. Interestingly, more than one Plant in a team reduces the team's overall likelihood of success, because they tend to pick holes in each other's ideas rather than develop their own.

3. **A good spread of mental abilities**. Oddly enough, it is important not only that there should be at least one very clever team member, and at least one other clever enough to provide stimulating discussion for the first, but also that some members of the team should be of lower mental ability. Dr Belbin suggests that this may be because their inability to compete with their cleverer colleagues for team roles leads them to find other roles in which they can shine, thereby creating a broader spread among the team as a whole.

4. **A spread in personal characteristics giving a wide coverage of team roles**. Teams that can accommodate most or all of the team roles perform better than others. Not only is there less of the friction that is caused by two or more people competing for the same role, but there is also a greater chance of having any given role that you might need.

5. **A good match between team members' attributes and their responsibilities in the team**. We tend to allocate people responsibilities according to their experience. But in the most successful teams, the members' responsibilities fit their team role profiles. It's no good putting a Plant in charge of finishing detailed tasks and tying up the loose ends – you just won't get the best results out of them.

6 **Recognition of imbalance in the team and the ability to adjust to it**. Teams that have this kind of self-awareness, and are prepared to adapt or change roles in order to build on their strengths or compensate for their weaknesses, are at an advantage.

A change of balance

It's worth noting that the best mix for a team can vary according to the task in hand. In the early stages of a project, when you are developing and honing ideas, you really need your Plant, Resource Investigator and Monitor Evaluator. A good Co-ordinator will be an excellent team or project leader to help these three work smoothly together. When you start to put your ideas into practice the Implementer is vital, along with the Team Worker – especially if things are getting at all difficult or fraught. By this stage you may find that the drive of a Shaper becomes important in moving the project along, and as you progress a Completer becomes vital to see the task through.

So different roles are important at different stages, and these can vary according to the project. Some people can even be a liability at certain times. You may find, for example, that your Plant is constantly trying to find ways to adapt and improve ideas beyond the point and after the date when changes are helpful. In this case it might be wise to distract the Plant with a new problem to solve, for example, so as to keep them out of the way while the rest of the team completes the current project.

Balancing team roles is, of course, less crucial for a team whose principal function is to operate a more or less steady and continuous process with little change over the years. But if the team operates in areas of rapid change in terms of the workforce, manufacturing techniques, products, markets or costs; or if their work is largely project orientated; or if there is competition, pressure and the need to make fast decisions, then it becomes vital to have all the different team skills available.

Working with smaller teams

Suppose you're running a team of four people. Which team roles are you supposed to manage without? Well, none of them necessarily. Everyone can play at least one secondary role, so you should be able to manage. And many teams don't need certain roles. If your team is effectively a think-tank, for example, you probably don't need a Completer. Many teams can manage without a Specialist. But beyond that, the types tend to divide into four whose preoccupation and orientation is to the world outside the team, and five who are chiefly concerned with what goes on inside the team:

- *Outward looking*: Co-ordinator, Plant, Resource Investigator, Shaper
- *Inward looking*: Implementer, Monitor Evaluator, Team Worker, Completer, Specialist.

Most people tend to be either outward or inward looking (extrovert or introvert) by nature. And successful teams tend to include at least one extrovert and one introvert. Beyond that, you may well find that each team member can take on two or even three roles each. For example, some Plants make excellent Co-ordinators, and some Implementers are excellent Team Workers and good Completers as well. If you are in a position to choose your team you need to select carefully, but it should be perfectly possible to build a successful team with fewer than nine members. In fact, Dr Belbin's research suggests that nine is, in any case, a little larger than the ideal team size. He suggests that in an ideal world you should aim for six people if you want to construct a co-operative team that works closely together.

The other consideration to bear in mind if you have to work with a small team is that you may not need certain roles at all. Most teams benefit from someone who can function as a Team Worker, and the majority need a Resource Investigator and an Implementer – but not all; it depends on the team's responsibilities and the number of members it has. If you're down to two people, you can probably manage without a Co-ordinator, for example. Or if your function is to implement another department's initiatives you may not need a Plant. And, as I mentioned before, many teams don't use any specialised technical skills or knowledge, and therefore don't need a Specialist.

Correcting an unbalanced team

This all sounds great, but you've inherited a team of three Plants and four Shapers and you can't just sack them all. So what can you do? Well, you have various options. You may find that one will solve your problem, or you may need to use a combination of two or more approaches:

1. **Reshuffle**. It sounds dramatic, but it may well be a good idea for two or more team members to swap jobs, or swap the bulk of their jobs. If this puts both of them into a role in which they are more likely to excel, the chances are they will both welcome it.

2 **Increase flexibility of functions in the team**. Find out which tasks each team member enjoys and performs well at. Then see if you can't divvy up some of them differently. This is different from swapping entire areas of responsibility. You give this person a bit of that one's job, and take away a bit of theirs to give to the other person, who is passing on one of their tasks to someone else. You need, of course, to be wary of removing from someone a responsibility that they both enjoy and are good at, and if they enjoy it but have no particular talent for it you need to be especially diplomatic – although there's a good chance that they will recognise the fact.

You may want to try this approach on a small scale first, just juggling round a few tasks to begin with, and one of the benefits of this approach is that it enables you to do this. If you have any team members who are very resistant to change this can be a less confrontational way to bring it about since you are only adjusting things a little at a time.

3 **Separate team members who clash**. What about those three Plants? It may be that you can subdivide your team into smaller working groups each with responsibility for a different project, or a different stage of the same project. Put one of your Plants into each working group, so that each of them has a challenge to themselves. If you can't separate certain team members who clash, make sure that whenever they get together in meetings or discussion groups there is someone conciliatory there as well, such as a Team Worker or a Co-ordinator.

4 **Transfer or swap with another team**. Maybe your colleague in the next department has a team whose performance is hampered because it doesn't contain a Shaper to galvanise all the Team Workers and Completers into action. If you swapped a suitable Shaper for a suitable Team Worker, the chances are that everyone would be a lot happier and both teams would perform better.

5 **Recruit**. This is not always an option of course. But there are times when you have the resources and a heavy enough workload to justify it, and adding a certain type to the team can make a huge difference. If you do take this route, it's a good idea to recruit someone who is a good example of the type you need, and whose self image lines up well with the view that others take of them.

Needless to say, once you have identified the team roles of all your team members, you should consider the team role requirements of the group every time you replace a member of staff who leaves or when you expand the size of your team as its workload or responsibilities grow. It can of course take a while to convert a badly composed team to a winning team, but these measures should help speed up the process.

Once you recognise that just about everyone has valuable strengths as well as allowable weaknesses, you realise that many people who underperform or disrupt the team are doing so because the organisation is not exploiting them fully – in a sense they are being let down by the company rather than the other way round. So if you decide to transfer someone to another team, or change their area of responsibility, make sure they appreciate that you're doing it in their interests as much as in the interests of the team. Explain the reasons to them, and let them know how their strengths can be better developed to everyone's benefit as a result of the changes.

Once you've identified the team role of everyone in your team, and got them working in the most suitable functions, you have constructed the foundations on which to build your great team.

If you want to know more about Meredith Belbin's work, team role analysis or team role workshops you can contact Belbin Associates Limited at 3–4 Bennell Cart, West Street Comberton, Cambridge CB3 7DS, UK or phone (01223) 264 975.

CHAPTER TWO

Motivation

Now you've assembled the ideal combination of people – or at least the best you can obtain – you need them to *want* to work, and to want the team to succeed. Broadly speaking, there are two kinds of motivation: short-term and long-term:

- **Short-term: you want your team members to approach the next task with enthusiasm.**
- **Long-term: you want them to stay with the team and consistently give their best.**

Everybody's different, as we said before, and understanding this is the key to motivation, because everyone is motivated in different ways. Your job is to find out what makes them all tick. This chapter will examine:

- **individual motivation and team motivation;**
- **which motivational techniques undermine team spirit and which help to build the group's identity;**
- **various types of reward and which type of person each approach is likely to work for;**
- **motivating people in difficult situations.**

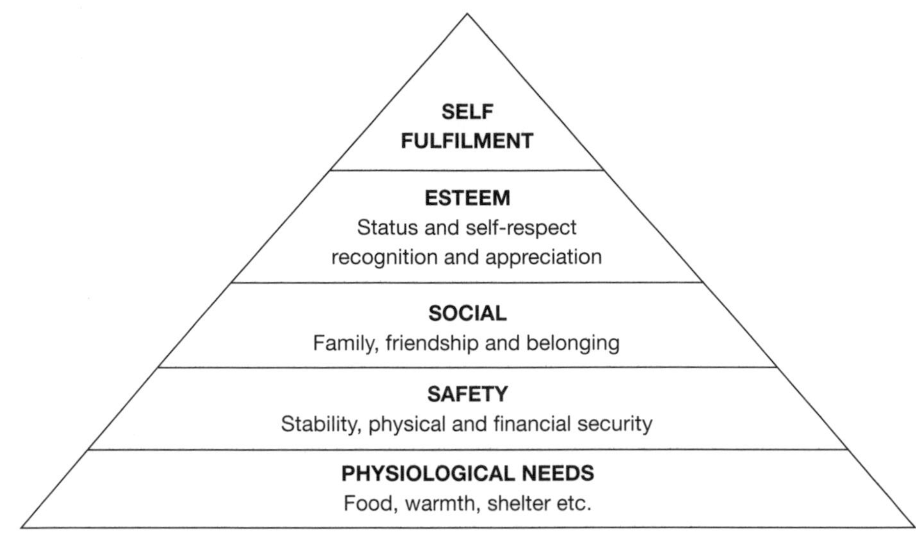

Maslow's hierarchy of needs

Motivation is all about satisfying people's wants and needs. In other words, once they feel that it is worthwhile doing something because of the satisfaction it will generate, they are motivated. There are certain basic needs that everyone shares – food, warmth and so on – which your team members' basic wages should satisfy. But once these needs are met, people start to look for more. Maslow's hierarchy of needs (see diagram) shows a pyramid with basic needs at the bottom, and a structure above that of other needs. The principle is that you cannot achieve any of these goals until you have established the ones below it as a foundation.

If your team members find that their jobs satisfy most or all of these needs, they will be highly motivated to work hard. If they perceive that hard work will lead to rewards that increase the supply of any of these needs – greater security, for example, or a stronger sense of self-fulfilment – they will be motivated to strive for these goals.

Some people interpret Maslow's hierarchy of needs to mean that everyone is motivated by the same things. That isn't the case. Perhaps at the bottom of the scale it's true that everyone needs to eat and sleep and so on. But as soon as you move up the scale, differences appear. Everyone needs security, for example, but some people need only minimal security, while others can have a guaranteed job for life and five pension schemes and still feel uneasy. Again, some people are naturally confident, and knowing they are doing a good job gives them all the self-esteem they need. Others need to be told constantly that they are performing well. Job satisfaction is a large part of self-fulfilment. Everybody might want it, but what constitutes a satisfying job for one person might seem totally unchallenging, or frustrating, to the next.

People don't start out motivated or demotivated. They are like a blank sheet of paper, ready to list the pros and cons of doing the job they do, or of performing specific tasks. It's all a question of whether the circumstances fit their particular needs. And that's the bit that's down to you. If you create the right environment, your team members will effectively motivate themselves.

Doing the filing

Pros (Motivating factors)	Cons (Demotivating factors)
Desk will be tidier	Takes time
Feeling of satisfaction	Boring
Boss will be pleased	Unchallenging
Easier and quicker to find things once it's done	Can't chat while doing it
Worth it to keep job which, on balance, is enjoyable	Frustrating because it will need doing again soon

The factors on the pros or cons side of the list will vary from person to person – some people, for example, really enjoy filing and find it a relaxing, therapeutic break from their other tasks. You will also find a difference between short-term and long-term motivating factors. Many people will be motivated to get the task in hand completed by factors such as:

- being able to go home on time
- getting a task they don't enjoy out of the way
- the satisfaction of completing a task they do enjoy
- the prospect of the appreciation they will earn for doing the job well
- wanting to retain a reputation for always delivering on time

and many more – not to mention individual motivating factors that go with specific jobs, like wanting to put the rubbish out because you can't stand the smell any longer.

The long-term factors that motivate people look a bit different – they tend to be more general and are often, though not always, more abstract. Here are a few examples:

- security
- money
- status
- recognition
- responsibility
- job satisfaction.

And there's one other motivating factor that isn't present in every group of people, but it's there in every great team. You can motivate people towards team needs and wants as well as personal ones. If you can generate that elusive team spirit, you'll find that the team members are motivated by the prospect of collective achievements and rewards. They will be proud to be associated with the team as a whole, and will actively want some successes, recognition and rewards for the whole team as well as for themselves individually.

Individual motivation

The long-term motivating factors, as we saw, are often quite abstract. But that doesn't mean that you can't supply those motivations in a specific, concrete way. Let's have a look at the most common factors which motivate people in the long term, and some of the concrete ways in which you can supply them.

Money

This one is fairly concrete to start with. There are a number of ways in which you can use money to motivate people:

- obviously you can give them a substantial salary; they'll want to work hard to make sure they hold on to a well-paid job;
- you can give them financial bonuses, or the prospect of promotion – with a concomitant rise in salary – if they perform well;

- people often respond well to suggestion schemes in which a successful idea will earn them a share in the profits it makes or the savings it accrues;
- maybe you could put them on a commission of some kind, or performance related pay (which we'll look at later in this chapter).

It's worth noting that when it comes to motivation, money is what is known as a 'hygiene factor'. If people think they're underpaid (usually relative to others) they are demotivated, but once they feel they are well enough paid most people won't feel any more motivated just because you pay them more – just as dirty loos demotivate, but once they're made clean and decent you can't increase motivation by adding gold-plated taps. Most complaints about money are precipitated by the discovery that someone the person thought was worth less than them is actually being paid more.

Security

For a lot of people who crave security, money is one of the key things that represents it. So some of the above will apply. The following also applies to such people:

- they often tend to be happier with a guaranteed income, and might rather have a lower salary they can be certain of than one that is dependent on their performance, even though it might work out higher. So they are likely to be wary of any kind of commission or performance related pay that means their basic wage is set at a lower level;
- they are likely to be interested in pension schemes, promising security for the future;
- they will be enthusiastic about anything that makes their contract more secure. If your organisation is in a line of business where a lot of people are on short-term or fixed-term contracts, you might consider a different system for these people if you can.

Status

The important thing here is not only to be valuable to the organisation, but to be seen to be valuable. Promotion is obviously a strong motivating factor for these people, and they like to work in organisations where there is plenty of opportunity for it. If there is nowhere to promote these people to, or they're not ready, or you want to keep them on the team, there are other ways of conferring status:

- give them a new job title;

- give them a bigger office;
- put them in charge of a prestige, high profile project;
- upgrade their company car – or at least give them a better parking space;
- these people are likely to see training as a way of preparing for new responsibilities or a step on the ladder to the next promotion, and they generally welcome the opportunity to learn new skills.

Recognition

There are lots of ways to show someone public appreciation for a job well done, which we'll look at later in the chapter when we discuss rewards. But it is important to let people know in advance that good work will be recognised:

- this will work automatically if your organisation or team has a regular system such as a column in the staff newsletter for recording successes, or an 'Employee of the Month' certificate pinned on the notice board;
- you could tell your team in advance that a specific project is important enough to merit an article in the newsletter, or even a chance of a story in the local press, if it's successful. Perhaps you could arrange that the MD will personally thank the team if they pull off the contract they're working on at the moment.

Responsibility

Some people get a buzz out of taking on greater responsibilities. It might be something to do with status, but it isn't for everyone. For some it is because of the challenge, but again this isn't always so. Some people like to feel in control, and for some it may be a matter of wanting more power. It helps to know which is the case (it might be a combination of factors), because this gives you a clue as to the kind of responsibility to give them:

- this is not just a matter of giving people extra tasks to perform; the point is to *delegate* those tasks. In other words, they take on not only the work but also the responsibility for seeing that it is done well;
- you will need to agree with the person what information, resources and equipment they need to do the job, and then provide them. Then keep out of their way until the job is done, unless they come to you for help.

There are, of course, certain provisos here to ensure that you don't end up with a disaster on your hands:

- make sure that you are both absolutely clear about the results you expect and the deadline for the job. Focus on results, not methods: you can specify the time, cost and quality, but let *them* choose, within these boundaries, how they want to achieve the agreed result;
- if you are concerned that they may find it difficult to complete the task successfully, set interim deadlines and targets, and plan regular review sessions to see how they are getting on. But leave them alone between these times unless they come to you;
- encourage them to ask questions and discuss any problems with you;
- support them if there are any problems over resources, such as access to equipment that they need to use – bear in mind the point made in the introduction about being the servant of the team;
- if the task or project is completed successfully, give full credit to the person you delegated it to. This is vital if you want them to continue to feel motivated to take on responsibility.

Job satisfaction

Many people are motivated by more than one factor of course, and most are motivated by the prospect of being satisfied by the job they do:

- people need to feel they are doing the job well in order to feel satisfied, so you need to be sure that people are as well suited as possible to the job they do. This is not just a matter of matching their skills and experience to the requirements of the job, but also making sure they are fulfilling a suitable team role in the group, as we discussed in Chapter 1;
- it's also important that people can see how their job fits into the scheme of things. If the tasks they perform are simply part of a larger task – for example they simply log details onto the computer, or just work on one section of the production line – make sure they understand why their part of the process is important to the success of the whole thing. We'll look at this in more detail in a moment.

Challenge

The following factors need to be taken into account when considering challenge as a motivator:

- some people derive huge personal satisfaction from proving to themselves or other people that they can achieve things that no one was quite certain they would manage;
- people need to be constantly stimulated with new targets and objectives;
- you may be able to give people completely new tasks to perform, to stretch them in a different way;
- people don't necessarily need responsibility. Of course responsibility is a challenge in itself and will be important for some, but for others it is only a minor factor;
- generally speaking people love to be trained because it enables them to take on new challenges.

If you're not sure what motivates each individual member of your team there's a simple way to find out. Ask them. Either discuss it with them, perhaps at their appraisal or separately, or give them a simple questionnaire to fill out:

Long-term motivation

Pros Motivating factors	Cons Demotivating factors

Key motivating factors

I know I said everyone was different, but nevertheless there are certain factors which motivate just about everyone – or lack of which demotivate everyone. Here are the most important guidelines to follow:

1 *The more your team members understand about their jobs, the reason for them and the value of them, the more motivated they will be.* Show them how their part fits in with the organisation as a whole. Don't just tell them once when they join the team; keep reinforcing it. Every so often take them round the offices or on a factory visit, and look for opportunities for them to visit departments or branches that are based on another site. You might even be able to organise the occasional job swap within the organisation, or ask if members of your team can help staff on the next exhibition stand – especially if their job rarely brings them into direct contact with customers. They'll enjoy themselves, enjoy the change, and understand their own role better.

Make sure they see the results of their labours too, especially if they don't work at the customer contact end of the operation. Take them to visit some of the retail outlets you sell through, or get a business customer to agree to let them come and see the equipment actually working in situ.

2 *Always set people clear and achievable targets.* Make sure these are agreed, rather than dictated, and review them regularly. If you don't know what your target is, how can you measure your performance? Remember school exams? You'd be told you had got 60 per cent and you'd be really pleased with yourself; then you'd discover that the top mark was 98 per cent and no one else had scored below 65 per cent. On the other hand if it had been, say, physics you would probably have come top if you'd managed 60 per cent.

Your team members need to know when they're doing well or badly. So everyone needs their own quantifiable performance targets, as well as team targets. And the more specific you are, the better; vagueness can be a powerful demotivator. Not only are people unclear as to what they are supposed to be achieving, but you will also be giving the impression that it doesn't really matter – which translates to your team members as *they* don't really matter.

You can think of this point and the previous one in terms of running a Blue Peter Appeal (if you remember them). These were the stages:

- they always told you right from the start how much money (or how many stamps or milk bottle tops) they were trying to raise, and why they needed it;
- each week they would tell you the total raised so far, and how many more weeks there were to go. And they'd remind you why this cause was worth supporting;
- at the end, they would have a big celebration on the programme (they always reached the target), and tell everyone how wonderful they were and how much difference it would make. They even rewarded special effort with a Blue Peter badge (I've still got mine);
- shortly afterwards, they would have a special report to show you what had been achieved as a result of all that effort ('Here's Whisky, one of the new guide dogs you helped pay for, leading her owner onto the bus...').

3 *Involve people.* Tell them everything you can about what's going on in the organisation. Ask them for suggestions and ideas, and help in solving problems. As part of this you must be seen to be listening: people will stop making suggestions if you never take them up. Of course some of the ideas may not seem that promising, but you can talk through the difficulties with the person who made the suggestion and perhaps arrive, jointly, at a better idea. Even if you can't usefully build on the original suggestion, at least the person will understand why and will feel you've listened – and their next idea may be more practicable.

This point is vital, because once people feel involved, they feel more associated with the project or the work of the team. If things go badly they feel a degree of responsibility, and when they go well they feel that some of the glory reflects onto them. This is largely what motivates them about feeling involved, and in order to encourage it you need to make sure that you always acknowledge their involvement in any success.

The role of the leader

This book is not about leadership; its focus is on the team rather than the leader. Nevertheless, as team leader, some of the factors in motivating your team members are down to your personal behaviour or attitude.

Handling mistakes

If people are in the right job and the right environment – which is your responsibility – they will be motivated, at least to some extent, and they will not work badly on purpose. This means that any mistakes they make are just that – mistakes. They will feel that they couldn't help it. If you reprimand them, shout at them or punish them, they will resent it as being unfair – after all they couldn't help it; it was a mistake. The only real effect this approach has is to make sure that next time, the person will do everything they can to stop you finding out about their mistakes.

It's far better to view mistakes as an opportunity to learn. Don't criticise people for their mistakes; sit them down and ask them how they think the mistake happened. Then discuss with them ways to prevent it recurring. Thank them for being honest enough to tell you about it. Next time they make a mistake (and there's less likely to be a next time this way), they'll feel comfortable enough to tell you about it. And that can make the difference between containing the problems it causes or letting them get out of hand. What's more, they'll respect you for acknowledging that it was a mistake but treating them with respect in the way you handled it. You can create an 'owning-up' culture by telling them your mistakes, and laughing about your own dreadful cock-ups in the past.

Of course some mistakes do recur frequently enough that they need to be handled more seriously, and these are dealt with in later chapters.

Mean what you say

It's very demotivating to be told one thing by someone whose actions suggest something quite different. At best it's confusing and at worst you get the impression that they don't trust you. Some managers will say 'This report is excellent! Thank you' and next thing you know, they're scribbling corrections all over it. Why do that if it's excellent? Or if it's not, why say it is? And if they're going to rewrite it however good it is, why bother making the effort next time?

Be positive

Focus on the plusses, not on the minuses. If you're going through a piece of work with someone that's not entirely up to scratch, the negative approach is: 'Well it could be worse, but we'd better talk about several things here that need improving.' Your poor team member will trudge away, head in hands, thinking 'I'm hopeless; that was a dreadful piece of work.' They won't feel it's worth trying any more, and their motivation will nosedive.

The positive approach is to say 'There's some good work here. You set about this in exactly the right way, and gave yourself a clear structure to work to. After that one or two aspects of the project got rather confused. If we go through them we can work out what happened so you don't have problems next time.' Once you've gone through it you can end by saying 'By the way, thanks for delivering it on time as usual. I can always rely on you to meet deadlines.' This time, they'll leave thinking 'I'm almost there. One or two points to practise and I'll be really good at this.' So always start and end on a good point.

In the same vein, always look forward and not back. Give the clear signal that when things go wrong you only look for the reasons because of the lessons they can teach for next time. In other words, don't go over past mistakes to allocate blame, but in order to improve future performance.

Be likeable

There is a myth that it doesn't matter whether your team like you or not so long as they respect you. Research demonstrates the opposite, however: if they like you they will learn faster, set higher standards for themselves and be more productive. That doesn't mean you have to be everyone's best mate, it just means that your team will be more motivated to work for someone they like. So be friendly and reasonably open about yourself, be polite, be generous about other people's successes, and let your team know that you like them.

Don't be tempted to sacrifice productivity in favour of being liked – it isn't necessary. If you have to be firm occasionally your team won't like you any less, so long as they can see the need for it.

Be polite

Don't tell your team what to do – ask them to do it. If you've built a well motivated team they won't need to be instructed, and they won't challenge you. It seems a small point, but anyone whose team leader never says please or thank you will tell you that it makes quite a difference. And if you're asking someone to do something that isn't really their job, make it clear that you know it's not their job: 'Robin, I know you're busy but Kim's not here today – please could you call production and check they're still on target for the Birmingham job?' That way, they won't feel taken for granted and they'll be happy to help.

Be generous

Relationships are two-way things, and it's no good expecting people to do something for you that you wouldn't do for them. There are always going to be times when you need someone on your team to stay late, or cover for someone else's job, or do something else that they aren't really paid to do. They will be far more motivated to co-operate on these occasions if they feel you'd do the same for them. So if it's humanly possible, be generous about giving them time off when there's a serious illness in their family, or letting them come in half an hour late when they've been let down on the school run and have to drop the kids off on the way to work.

Team motivation

Since teams are made up of individuals, you need to make sure that you tailor your motivational techniques to the particular people you have in your team. But it's also important to motivate the team collectively, in order to build and maintain the group as a team and not just a collection of individuals working together.

Everyone is motivated to some degree by being successful, and they will be motivated collectively by being part of a sucessful team. So you need to create an environment in which the team can achieve this together. This means that they need to score successes that they could not have done individually. In order to do this, everyone needs a clearly defined function and role in the team, so that when a project goes well they can all see that it just couldn't have happened without Kate's ideas, Robin's contacts, the superb planning and scheduling that Andy came up with, your knack with handling other departments, Kim's skill at negotiating and so on.

Even smaller projects and tasks can be handled by two or three people with complementary skills, so it is still apparent that the success is collective. This gives you the opportunity to recognise each person's individual contribution, but also recognise the team's achievement as a team. This may sound obvious, but team leaders often ask people who possess similar skills to work together on projects, so that when the project is completed each one feels that they could have done the whole thing alone.

To motivate the team as a team, you need to put some hard, and often creative, thought into which combinations of people to put together on projects and tasks so that they each recognise their own importance, and each other's, in achieving it.

We'll come onto the subject of rewarding good work later, but it's worth saying at this point that it's vital for motivating the team that you always reward team achievements collectively. Of course you will want to praise or thank each member individually for their own contribution, but any reward must be a shared one.

Many of the key motivating factors we looked at earlier can be provided collectively, such as by keeping people informed of what's going on and putting their role in context. Talk to the team as a group rather than individually when you can, and take them on factory visits or to exhibitions as a team whenever you can. Set team objectives and team targets, as well as individual ones, that cannot be met unless everyone pulls together.

The physical environment

We said earlier that you need to create the right environment in order for people to be motivated. Don't forget to include in this the physical environment. People who work in dingy basements that haven't been redecorated for thirty years do not tend to be as productive as people who work in clean, well lit, freshly decorated buildings. Keeping the surroundings bright and pleasant is not as high a priority with many managers as it should be.

But when it comes to planning the workspace, the design you adopt can affect team motivation and team spirit. If everyone is shut away in offices they won't feel like such a cohesive group as if they work in an open-plan space. It's far better to keep everyone in the same physical area, and keep the space as open as possible. Try to arrange things so that everyone sees each other quite frequently throughout the day, even if they're simply walking past someone who is busy talking on the phone. It often helps to put equipment everyone uses, such as the fax, photocopier or coffee machine somewhere central for this reason. Sometimes this can prove mildly disruptive, but often it doesn't.

People who are well motivated want to reach their targets and get the best results and they won't spend 45 minutes chatting over the photocopier every day. A five minute chat – if they can spare the time – is often a good thing. Not only does it help build relationships in the team, but you will also find, if you listen to these sorts of conversations, that they are sometimes used as an informal method of ironing out problems in the team. You might overhear 'I can't believe how drunk I was on Friday night...', but you might equally well hear 'It took four days to process those customised orders last week. I was wondering, if the orders went to you *first*, and then you passed them to me ...'.

Some of the work of the team may need to be done in private – such as meetings with customers or suppliers – and often the best solution is to have meeting rooms that anyone in the team can use for this purpose. Also, some people work better alone and in a quiet atmosphere, and of course you need to recognise these people's personal styles of work to get the best from them. But to keep the team together, it can be better to meet these people half way: give them a desk in the open-plan area, but allow them to spend an hour or two a day in a meeting room concentrating on the work they most want privacy or peace and quiet for.

One of the latest team building trends is known as 'hot desking'. The idea is that no one has their own desk – when you arrive in the morning you simply pick any desk at random to work from for the day. The idea is that as you all share all the desks it builds team spirit. You might think this is a little impractical, but it can work well in some situations. For example if you have a team of telephone sales staff whose desks have nothing on them but a computer terminal, it could be perfectly workable. Why not try it for a week and see how the team feels about it? Do allow, though, for the fact that some people need the security of a personal desk with their own potted plant on it and so on, and can be demotivated by this kind of approach to team building.

One other point about the working environment. Most people like a change, and it can stimulate creativity. Look for opportunities to move around the building, or even beyond it. If you're holding a team planning meeting, find a quiet spot in the local park if the weather's good. Or hold your next brainstorming session on the roof. (But it might be wiser to resist pressure to hold all your meetings down at the pub.)

Undermining the team

There are certain mistakes you should take special care to avoid because they will not only demotivate the individual members of the team but they will also undermine the team spirit you are trying to build (I make no apology for repeating certain crucial points I have mentioned earlier):

1 **Generating friction**. Make sure you don't throw people into close working relationships who you know rub each other up the wrong way. Even the best teams have certain combinations of people that don't gel as well as others. If you need to bring them together – and you may do to maximise the team's performance – take precautions to minimise the friction. Don't make them spend more time in each other's company than necessary, and don't ask them to work together for longer than you really need to. For example, if you need them to plan a project together, have a reshuffle after the planning stage is complete and give them separate areas of responsibility. It is also wise to have a third person, for example a Team Worker of the type described in Chapter 1, working with the other two, if only to keep the peace.

2 **Unfairness**. If your team sees you as being unfair – even if you think the accusation is unjustified – you have a problem that will push the team apart. If they think you always give the best projects to one person, or someone is getting a bigger bonus than everyone else, you need to do something about it. It's always best to be open, and discuss it with everyone. Don't leap in and justify yourself; start by asking them why they feel it's unfair and what they think you could have done instead. This kind of approach should resolve the problem, but of course ideally you need to guard against the situation arising in the first place.

3 **Devaluing the currency of praise**. There are some aspects of motivation you can't really overdo, such as keeping people informed and involving them. But there are some, and in particular praise and rewards, that lose their effect if you are overgenerous with them. Certainly good work deserves praise. But if someone performs moderately well and you say 'That is absolutely brilliant – first class! Where would we be without you?', you're going to be lost for something appropriate to say when they perform brilliantly. So match the praise to the achievement. A simple 'Thanks – good work' is fine.

Equally, when work is below standard, you must say so (in a positive way, as we saw earlier). Otherwise they won't respect you or your judgement, and any praise will become meaningless. A useful guide to follow is to be specific, which is far more helpful for your team and has more meaning. For example 'Well done. It's not easy calming down a customer who is that angry, and you handled it extremely well.' It's even more effective if you talk about it for a bit too: 'What was it you said to calm him down enough to explain his problem properly?'

4 **Rewarding individuals for team achievement**. This is worth repeating; where a success has been achieved because the team worked together, you must underline this in any reward you give. Otherwise you are implying that individual performance was more important to the overall achievement than team work.

Building team spirit

Obviously this includes the opposite of these points we have just covered; you need to minimise friction, be seen to be fair, match your praise and rewards to the achievement, and reward the team for team successes. Here are a few more techniques and approaches to consider:

1 **Encourage team members to support each other**. If someone needs advice or guidance find another team member equipped to provide it instead of always doing it yourself. And try to eliminate unnecessary job demarkation. For starters, have a rule that if anyone passes an empty desk and the phone is ringing they should answer it – even if all they can do is take a message. And if one team member has an urgent task to complete, get all available hands on deck for 15 minutes to get it done. Of course this would be disruptive if you did it all the time, but once in a while when it's really useful it helps to create a feeling of mutual support.

2 **Train the team together**. Of course this isn't always appropriate, but group training sessions do bring people together. Any form of awareness training about the organisation as a whole and the team's role in it is particularly useful and should be done as a group.

3 **Put different people in charge of different projects**. This keeps the team fluid and encourages mutual respect. It also helps your team members to recognise that people are in charge of tasks, not in charge of each other for the sake of it. Obviously your more experienced or more skilled people will be in charge of the more demanding projects, but at the other end of the scale you can put the newest and least experienced member of the team in charge of the stationery cupboard or the fax machine. The important thing is that you back them up if necessary, and publicly support their authority over their own area – if there are any stumbling blocks you sort them out in private. And you absolutely must toe the line along with everyone else – just because you're the team leader you can't override the

stationery re-ordering system or make promises to customers that no one else is allowed to.

4 **Give your team confidential information**. This makes people feel that you trust them, but there are certain rules you need to follow to make it work or it can backfire on you:

- tell everyone in the team, not just project leaders or managers;
- there is some information it isn't fair to give people. For example it is a lot to ask of sales staff to give them information about new products and then expect them not to breathe a word to their customers. Any information which would warrant a serious inquiry if it leaked out is an unfair burden to place on anyone who doesn't need to know it;
- don't give your team confidential information about other members of staff ('The chief accountant isn't really on annual leave, he's been suspended on the grounds of suspected embezzlement');
- don't claim that information is secret when it's not. Your team members will feel they've been taken for a ride when they hear it from somewhere else;
- tell them when the information stops being confidential. If they've known for months about the new product developments, tell them that the press launch is coming up and they don't have to keep quiet about it any longer.

The kind of confidential information to give your team includes such things as new product plans, financial information about the organisation or impending administrative changes.

5 **Treat *everyone* as part of the team**. Larger teams especially often include secretaries and PAs, who can sometimes feel left out if you're not careful. These people perform a crucial role, and should always be treated with the same respect as the rest of the team. With the best will in the world they are sometimes excluded from training or team meetings or activities. What's more, because of the traditional view of these roles as being 'junior' or 'less important' they are often more sensitive about being included and will notice when you treat them differently from the rest of the team.

It makes a difference to everyone in the team if you make sure that secretaries and PAs are fully included. You can't create a feeling that you're all pulling together when there are clearly people there who aren't – because they're not being given the chance.

One of the biggest problems with this is that secretaries and PAs are usually the ones left to 'hold the fort' whenever the team is meeting or in training. But this is often unnecessary when you come to look at it; perhaps you're leaving two people to look after things when one would do and the other could join the rest of the team. They could take it in turns. Or perhaps someone else isn't that crucial at this particular meeting and could answer the phones instead. Of course there are times when it has to be the secretary or PA who holds the fort. That's why you need to make sure that you don't allocate that role to them unnecessarily.

There are also times when you're organising a team reward of some kind for good work – perhaps you're taking the team out to lunch – and someone has to stay behind to keep things ticking over. The best way to handle this is to offer a slightly more tempting reward to whoever stays behind, for example a free dinner for two at a local restaurant so they can go with their partner. Throw this offer open to everyone, and if there's more than one volunteer draw names from a hat.

Different types of reward

Motivation is all about creating the right atmosphere for people to work productively. Rewards come later, *after* they've done the work. Of course rewards are part of motivation because people know, or at least hope, that they will get them. And each reward you give affects the individual or team motivation for the next task. This is an important point to bear in mind. If you give someone a very small reward in recognition of a huge achievement, they will be less motivated to perform so well in future ('I brought in an extra £50,000 of new business last year, and all the thanks I got was a bottle of cheap plonk'). So make sure the reward fits the achievement.

One other general point about rewards: they must be consistent. If you gave Michael a bottle of wine last month to thank him for working over the weekend, you'd better give Judith one for working this weekend. *You* might have forgotten about last month, but Judith might not. Equally, if you cracked open the champagne last time the team beat their monthly sales record, you'd better do it again next time. Otherwise the signal you're sending out is that you no longer care as much about the sales figures as you did.

Individual rewards

In theory one could look at individual personality types and predict what kind of rewards would motivate them. You'd probably be reasonably accurate but you'd make a few mistakes. Some people are surprisingly untrue to type. And it's important that you should match the reward accurately to the person. What I have done below therefore is not to list personality types, but the factors which motivate people. Once you've established that (bearing in mind that most people are motivated by more than one factor) you can come up with appropriate rewards quite easily; you'll find several suggestions listed in the table below.

So how are you going to find out what motivates your team members? The easiest way is to ask them, perhaps at their appraisal, or perhaps during training and development sessions. When it comes to specific rewards (a bunch of flowers or a box of chocolates?), you can always ask their colleagues' advice as well. And take notice of their general conversation. Do they enjoy gardening? Or wish they could spend more time with their kids? All these things are worth making a mental note of, as potential ideas for rewards.

Matching rewards with motivating factors

Motivating Factor	Suggested reward
Praise	Everyone likes to be told they've done well, whatever other reward they may also get. And virtually everyone likes some kind of public recognition when they've done especially well. You could send them a memo congratulating them, and copy it to senior management and the MD. Or announce their success in the newsletter. Or at a staff meeting (but don't forget that a few people find this really embarrassing and uncomfortable). Maybe you could give them an Employee of the Month certificate to pin up next to their desk. Or you could go for something a bit different – have the boss's Bentley pick them up and take them to work every day for a week.
Thanks	Again, most people like a personal thank you – for something a little bit special, a card they can keep on their desk with a message thanking them is a nice touch. And often the achievement warrants a gift as a reward as well. If this is personally chosen with their

Motivating Factor	Suggested reward
	interests in mind it will be worth more to them. Perhaps they're chocoholics, or love flowers, or maybe they'd appreciate theatre tickets. Or you could take them to lunch, maybe with a couple of colleagues of their choice. Or you could arrange for their car to be washed during office hours (if you don't check with them first, be sure they're the type that likes surprises). Or give them an extra hour for lunch. If their family is important to them give them a couple of bonus days' holiday, or a three day weekend. Almost anything goes – it just takes a bit of thought.
Money	People will appreciate an extra bonus even more than the praise you give them. Or offer them a small commission on top of their salary.
Status	Promotion is generally a reward for long-term performance rather than short-term achievement. But you could change someone's job title to something that they feel sounds more impressive. Or reward them for good work by putting them in charge of a prestigious new project.
Freedom	Some people, particularly creative or slightly unorthodox types, set a great deal of store by personal freedom. If they prove their value, you could reward them by agreeing some kind of teleworking or flexitime arrangement. Or give them tasks or responsibilities that mean they get out of the building more often.
Responsibility	If these people do well, offer them a new area of responsibility, or the prospect of it: 'You really made Amanda feel at home when she first joined the team. I was thinking of asking you to be responsible for inducting new people into the team in future. How would you feel about it?' Just one point – if you promise something for the future, remember when it comes to it without having to be reminded.

Motivating Factor	Suggested reward
Challenge	These people respond well to something along the lines of 'You've achieved such good results on the ABC project, I wondered if you'd like to take charge of the XYZ job when it comes up next month?' Or 'Do you fancy learning about fleet management? If we take on many more delivery vehicles I'm going to need someone to oversee them properly. After your recent work I think you'd be very capable with a bit of training, and there's a good course coming up next month.'

Team rewards

When the team does well, or works particularly hard, you need to give a joint reward as we've already seen. This underlines the importance of the team's collective contribution. This can cover anything from buying a box of cream cakes for them to share at the end of a busy week, to treating them all to a trip to the theatre or a smart restaurant when they complete a major project successfully.

Everyone in the team must have an equal share in any team reward. If you bring in a case of wine for them at Christmas, everybody gets the same number of bottles. If you give the extra one to your most senior team member you imply that everyone else is less important; you have to make sure there isn't an extra one. Incidentally, having said earlier that you should not reward people individually for team achievements, bear in mind that there is a huge psychological difference between putting a box of wine somewhere communal and saying 'That's for all of you to share', and putting a single bottle on each person's desk.

Make it fun

There's another, vital motivating factor we haven't mentioned yet: fun. If people are enjoying themselves they will be more productive and stay longer in the job. Aim for a happy relaxed atmosphere, and when people laugh share the joke, don't frown disapprovingly. One of the best ways to achieve this in a team is to hold friendly competitions, either between team members or get the whole team competing against its own previous best performance. It's important to keep this light and friendly, and when team members are competing against each other – for example to see who generates most sales this month – make the prize fairly small so there's no serious ill feeling among the losers. A bottle of wine, for example, or permission to have a lie-in next Monday morning.

If your team members are likely to become over-competitive, hold a competition that relies entirely on luck but can't be won without working hard. For example, you could give a prize to whoever answers the phone to the highest number of customers whose surnames begin with the letter 'F'.

Where the team is competing with itself, you can have a lot of fun. Suppose you're trying to get more responses to a mailshot than you've ever had before. Every morning when the post is opened you can give the latest bulletin: 'It's looking good – we're 25 responses ahead of our previous best at this stage.' As the numbers tot up things can get quite tense. Keep this tension going – it adds to the fun. Every morning ask whoever opens the post 'How are we doing? What's the latest score?' You could even put up a blackboard and chalk up the results each day under the heading of 'latest score'. When you hit a new record, take everyone to lunch that day. Or if you've just set a new weekly sales record on Friday afternoon, crack open the champagne.

Some ideas for rewards

Here are a few suggestions for team rewards, both large and small. None of them may be quite right for your team, but they should give you a starting point for coming up with your own ideas:

- cream cakes all round
- a team drink after work
- a team lunch
- a team outing – to a trade show to see the company's exhibition stand, or a boat trip down the river
- an office treat – spoil them at work: arrange a cooked breakfast for them
- redecorate the workplace so it's brighter and more pleasant to work in
- buy more comfortable chairs for the meeting room
- give them a better coffee machine, or a cold drinks dispenser.

Motivating in difficult situations

So far we've looked at motivation in fairly standard, average circumstances. But there are some situations which make it much harder to keep people motivated. So before concluding the chapter, let's have a look at some of the commonest difficulties.

Motivating temps and part-timers

This is actually nothing like as difficult as many people think; the solution is very simple: treat them in the same way as full-timers:

- pay part-timers the same rate pro rata as you do full-timers;
- when you have temps working on the team, make an effort to see that everyone knows their name. Use it yourself, especially in front of others;
- follow the same guidelines about keeping them informed and involving them;
- include them in team activities and team rewards;
- give them individual rewards and bonuses when their performance deserves it;
- if you set a good example, the rest of the team will follow it and treat temps and part-timers with the same respect as the other colleagues.

Motivating a team that's never there

It's hard to build and maintain team spirit among people who never see each other: sales engineers who are always on call, regional managers spread around the country or sales staff out on the road. However, these are useful pointers:

- the key thing is that these people *have* to meet as a team sometimes: once a week if you can manage it, but at least once a month;
- make sure you stay in regular touch with them all, by phone if necessary. If there's no reason to ring, do it anyway – tell them you're calling to keep in touch and see if they need anything, or to give them a bit of company news;
- encourage contact between them in twos and threes. For example, if Angela rings you for advice on a subject you know is one of Brian's strong areas, say 'The best person for you to talk to is Brian – he's a real expert on that and I'm sure he'll tell

you what you want to know.' This not only keeps the team members in contact with each other, it also encourages mutual respect for each other's expertise. For this reason, it's important not to put everybody onto Brian all the time or it undermines the rest of the team. Find an opportunity to tell Brian 'Angela knows that customer better than I do. Why not give her a ring and she'll fill you in on the history';

- see if you can improve informal communications – start a team news sheet, or a noticeboard if you all share the same site;
- go out of your way to promote team activities, team lunches and drinks after work;
- train the team as a single group if you possibly can;
- if you have one or two team members working at a fixed site who see more of the rest of the team than everyone else, get them on your side. Explain that you want to create a team feeling, and ask them to help. For example, ask them to encourage contact between other team members, and refer them to each other for help or advice rather than passing them on to you every time.

Motivating people to accept difficult or unpopular decisions

You can usually make people go along with decisions they don't like, by giving them no choice. But they're unlikely to put everything they've got into making such decisions work. So what you really want to do is to get them on your side. They may still not *like* the decision, but on balance they can see the sense and they want to make it work – and that's motivation. Here's the technique:

- once you've outlined the basic intention, the first thing to do is to ask your team to give you their views. Listen to them, and let them know you're listening;
- demonstrate that you can see they have a case – it's very important psychologically to acknowledge that their attitude is a valid one. For example: 'I can see that if we took on the sales operation in Scotland and Ireland it would increase your workload a great deal ...';
- let them see that you really listened to their arguments by referring to points they have made: 'Those of you on the road would have a lot more travelling to do, and it would give you less time with your families. And those of you based here would have to deal with a lot more paperwork';

- offer a compromise if necessary, so that they feel you're meeting them half way. 'We could reorganise the territories to minimise travelling, and we could make sure that everyone spends two consecutive days here at least once a fortnight. As far as the extra paperwork is concerned, we could take someone on part-time to help deal with that';
- give them a good reason why your decision is more effective (avoid value judgements like 'better'): 'It's more cost effective for the organisation as a whole to centralise sales, and this is the most logical place to run the sales operation from. We'll also be able to pool information and spot trends far quicker if we're dealing with a wider market, which should help us to achieve our objectives.' Ultimately, people aren't there to work for you or even for the team, but in order to accomplish the task. So the reason for something is never 'Because that's my decision' or 'Because it's not fair on Robin if we don't' but 'Because we can't reach our target/keep within budget/maintain quality/meet the deadline if we don't'.

Keeping motivation going when the pressure's on

It's easy for resentment to build up when you're asking the team to work harder than usual. Here are a few key guidelines for motivating your team to meet your demands without losing their enthusiasm:

- let them know why it's necessary for them to work at this pace or under these conditions; don't assume it's obvious because it may not be;
- acknowledge that they're working under increased pressure. This doesn't mean that you have to apologise or do anything about it, but they need to know that you're aware of it;
- work as hard or harder than you're asking them to; always be the last to leave at the end of the day;
- make sure you can justify everything you ask them to do when they're under pressure. After all, how would you feel if you had worked through your lunch break, and then expected to spend the afternoon tidying up the filing cabinet? If the team is putting in extra effort, only ask them to do vital or urgent tasks;
- if you're asking your team members to do something they're not technically obliged to – like working on a Saturday morning – make it easy for them to refuse. This will

actually make it more likely that they will agree to do it. Treat it as a favour, and be appreciative when they say yes, and they know it will score them brownie points. If you act as though they ought to do it they'll be resentful, and they won't feel their contribution will be recognised;

- keep the atmosphere fun and friendly. Just because everyone's under pressure try not to let them lose their sense of humour.

SUMMARY

1 Everyone is motivated by different factors – find out what they are for each member of your team.

2 Your attitude can encourage motivation:
- handle mistakes positively and fairly
- mean what you say
- be positive
- be likeable
- be polite
- be generous.

3 Motivate your team as a team, as well as motivating its members individually.

4 You can build team spirit by:
- minimising friction
- being seen to be fair
- matching rewards to the achievement
- rewarding the team collectively for team successes
- encouraging team members to support each other
- training the team together
- putting different people in charge of different projects
- giving the team confidential information
- treating *everyone* as part of the team.

5 Reward people in ways that suit their personal interests and individual motivating factors.

6 Make sure everyone has fun.

CHAPTER THREE

People problems

Some people can be difficult to work with, and we'll look at how to cope with this kind of team member in the next chapter. Most people are not usually a problem in themselves, however, but they can become involved in problem situations. For example their work may suffer because of personal factors that are pulling them down, or they may not handle stress very well. These things, if not addressed, can start to affect the morale of others around them, and eventually drag down the performance of the whole team. This chapter examines:

- **how to recognise that a team member is having personal problems;**
- **the ground rules for counselling people at work, and the options for dealing with the problem;**
- **how to cope with stress in individual team members (we'll look at team stress in Chapter 5).**

Recognising the problem

Suppose one of your team members starts arriving at work late on a fairly regular basis, having always been punctual in the past. What do you think might cause this? Here are a few possibilities:

1. They have been feeling very run down lately and find it increasingly hard to get up in the mornings.

2 The bus timetable has been rescheduled and they're still getting the hang of it.

3 They have always hated getting up early, and recently they have been doing so well at work that they reckon they can get away with taking the odd liberty without getting into trouble.

4 Their partner has left them and they have had to take over doing the school run two mornings a week, which makes them late.

5 There are roadworks on the route to work at the moment, and the delays are unpredictable.

Some of these causes are easier to resolve than others. As far as causes 2, 3 and 5 are concerned, one could reasonably argue that the team member should make more effort – to follow the bus timetable, get up in the mornings, or leave more time to allow for the roadworks.

But causes 1 and 4 are not quite so straightforward; the solution is not so obvious. These are areas where your team member could probably use some help or at least understanding from you.

But you don't actually know what the cause is yet – all you know is that they keep turning up late for work. However, the range of causes above (and there could be plenty of others, of course) should demonstrate that the mere fact that someone's late for work doesn't *necessarily* mean that they are 'to blame' in the traditional sense. They may have personal problems that need addressing. In other words, the lateness is only a symptom; there is a more complex underlying problem.

There are numerous problems that are often seen as signs of laziness, carelessness or bad attitude that could well be caused by personal problems over which the person has only limited control, or no control at all. Here are a few examples:

- drop in productivity
- deadlines being missed
- absenteeism
- bad temper, irritability
- lack of enthusiasm
- shoddy work
- negative attitude
- time wasting

- poor communication with others
- being quiet or distant.

Ah but, you might say, some people are naturally unenthusiastic or bad communicators and it doesn't mean anything. And you'd be right – which leads us on to the next question: how can you tell when one of your team is having problems that you could help ease?

The warning signs

Most people don't like to broadcast details of their personal problems – if they did, your job would be far easier. As it is, they're not going to come and tell you when things are going badly away from work; you're going to have to see it for yourself.

Some people are always prone to be late for work, some are naturally quiet and some are always irritable. So when do these signs indicate a deeper problem, and when do they mean little or nothing? The key factor is *change*. You need to notice when someone produces uncharacteristically shoddy work, or when a naturally enthusiastic person starts to adopt a negative outlook.

Sometimes you will notice this and you will know what causes it. Perhaps someone's productivity has dropped because there's been a change in work procedures and it's taking them a while to adapt. Maybe they are being quieter or more distant than usual because their work is particularly challenging at the moment and they don't have time for chatting or going to the pub at lunchtime. Be careful, though, not to *assume* that you know the cause. It's always safer, if you're in any doubt, to treat the matter as if there were a personal problem to deal with, until you're sure that everything is OK.

You may also be alerted to people's problems by the grapevine. This is not so much a matter of idle gossip; usually what happens is that a concerned colleague will let you know that someone's having problems because they hope that you can help. If this is the case, you obviously need to protect this person's confidence when you tackle the matter. The best way to do this is to start looking for warning signs yourself once someone else has alerted you to the situation. Otherwise, if by any chance your informant got their information wrong, you're going to be in a very uncomfortable situation when you start talking to the person you believe has a problem: 'I understand one of your parents is seriously ill?' 'No – they're both on a scuba-diving holiday in Florida. Who's been telling you this?'

Why bother?

Some people question what their team members' personal problems have got to do with them. Wouldn't it be better to keep out of it altogether; surely it's none of their business? And some people consider it somehow soft – it doesn't matter what's going on in their team members' private lives, it's part of their job to make sure it doesn't interfere with work.

It's true that in a sense your team members' private lives are none of your business, and certainly nothing, including poor performance at work, gives you the right to pry into details of it that your team member doesn't want to discuss. But very often they are more than happy to discuss the problem. They may not volunteer to talk about it because they're too proud, or they think you're too busy, or they're worried you'll think they can't cope, or because *they* think it's not your problem and they've no right to dump it on you. But they'll have realised that it's spilling over into the workplace and affecting their performance or their behaviour, and they will be glad of the opportunity to talk round ways of solving the problem. It may be that they actually *can't* solve it without your help, because they need you to approve or authorise a particular course of action – such as starting work half an hour later for a few weeks while they sort out someone to do the school run for them.

As far as being 'soft' is concerned, it's in your own interests and that of your team to do your best to resolve these problems. If you don't:

- the team member's productivity is likely to fall;
- their morale will drop, often taking other members of the team down with it;
- they are likely to become error prone, as their mind is preoccupied with the problem and not the task in hand;
- their behaviour will change, usually for the worse. In general they will either become moody, irritable and short-tempered, or they will withdraw and become quiet and distant.

Clearly, none of these outcomes is in the interests of the individual, the team or the tasks in hand. This list might seem rather extreme, but many seemingly minor problems can eventually reach this state if they are not addressed. It's terribly important to deal with things early, before they get out of hand.

Dealing with the problem

So, Peter's started turning up late to work two or three times a week. Not very late, but it's not like him to be late at all. Being a good manager, you've considered the possibility that it may not be plain laziness; there could be another problem. You've started watching his behaviour and he does seem a little more distracted than normal – not quite so eager as usual to be in the thick of things. Aha! It's a fair guess that there could be more to Peter's problem than meets the eye. Better do something about it, then. Um...what, exactly?

This is where a lot of managers, quite understandably, get a bit stuck. You probably got your job because of your abilities in organising, setting objectives and targets, motivating people and a number of other related skills. And your training since has probably concentrated on developing those areas. Now suddenly you're supposed to be a professional counsellor as well.

Well, the good news is that counselling skills are a lot easier to learn than you might think. And the most important things are all about what not to do. So as long as you avoid the worst mistakes, which we'll look at in a moment, you can't go that far wrong.

Counselling

The idea of counselling, in its simplest terms, is to talk to the person with the problem and arrive at a solution. That's all there is to it. But there are a few guidelines to follow through to make sure that they are willing to talk, and to ensure that the end solution is one that will work.

Setting the scene

If you rush up to someone who's in the middle of an urgent task, surrounded by several colleagues, and say 'You're not looking too happy. What's your problem?' they are unlikely to want to answer you. Obviously that's an extreme example, but it illustrates the importance of creating a relaxed and private setting for a counselling interview. Here are the most important points to consider:

- arrange a time that suits you both, when you can set aside *at least* half an hour;
- make sure you can meet in private;

- there must be *absolutely no interruptions*. If necessary, find another office than your own and don't let anyone know where you are, or even go for a walk with the person. Allowing interruptions implies that you don't consider the person's problems to be important;
- move the furniture (if necessary) so it is comfortable and arranged in a friendly, relaxed way. No one wants to open up and talk freely when they're sitting facing you across a desk, or when you're standing over them while they sit on an uncomfortable office chair. The ideal is a couple of easy chairs arranged round a coffee table;
- start by offering the person a cup of tea or coffee. Not only does it set up a relaxing, unhurried atmosphere, it's also a friendly gesture. Peter's probably been wondering for days when you're going to tackle him about his lateness for work, and this is an indication that he can relax – you're not about to give him a rollocking.

Discussing the problem

Now you're sitting with the person, in your easy chairs, how are you going to start the conversation? The best approach is to outline the problem that you can see, and acknowledge that there might be an underlying problem that you can't see. For example: 'Peter, I've noticed that you've been arriving at work later than usual recently. Can you tell me the reason?'

This is where you will find out whether, in fact, Peter simply hasn't been allowing enough time for the roadworks on the way to work. Or, as we saw earlier, you guessed at an explanation for a change in behaviour but didn't want to make assumptions. In that case this is where you discover that Peter is quieter than usual because he's focusing on a challenging piece of work. No harm done, and you can talk to Peter about leaving home earlier in the mornings, or ask him how he's getting on with the new project he's working on.

However, if you remember you had been astute enough earlier to notice that Peter was also quieter and more distant than usual, the likelihood is that he will respond by telling you that there *is* another problem. He won't necessarily come straight out with it but even a total silence would imply that the problem isn't simply the roadworks; you can be fairly sure you're into a proper counselling session here.

If Peter doesn't open up instantly (which is quite likely) you'll need to encourage him. Try saying something along the lines of 'I wonder if there's a problem I don't know about?' or 'If you can give me a clue as to what the problem is, I might be able to do something to help'.

One invaluable tip here is not to be afraid of silence. If Peter doesn't respond there's a temptation to speak again to fill the gap. But since you spoke last, the onus is on Peter, if anyone, to speak next. So just wait. If he's gone completely silent and is looking upset, just say 'It's OK there's no hurry. Take your time' and then shut up. Don't be embarrassed by the silence: there's nobody else there but Peter and if it's not bothering him, why should it bother you?

Sooner or later Peter will start to speak, once he knows that you're trying to help. Once he opens up and explains that his partner has left and he's coping with the children, there are certain stages you need to guide the conversation through:

1 **Acknowledge the person's feelings**. Reassure them that their response to the situation is valid; deep down, they're nervous you're going to say 'Is that all? What on earth are you making a fuss about?' Bear in mind that you may think that a team member's problem is minor, and you really may wonder what all the fuss is about. But it is *their* feelings you have to consider, because they are the one who has to deal with the situation. Your attitude to the problem isn't relevant. So reassure them with comments like 'No wonder you're finding it difficult to cope' or 'That must be a real strain for you.' It often helps to boost people's self-respect by saying something such as 'I'm surprised you've been coping as well as you have'. Don't be insincere, but if you find something in their response to be complimentary about, say so.

One word of warning here: avoid telling anyone that you understand how they feel. You don't, and they know it. Some people may not mind – later on in the conversation they might even ask you to say it ('you do understand, don't you?') but some people are upset and even angered by it. So err on the side of caution and don't say it unless you are 'asked' to. You might say to Peter 'I understand. Kim left me five years ago – I know what you're going through.' But it could be completely different for Peter. You can't know that the circumstances are the same, or that he feels about his partner exactly how you felt about Kim. Anyway, you're different people – perhaps he bottles things up while you're more inclined to trash the kitchen. Once again, we're all different – and we don't understand. Of course you're only trying to help, but a significant number of people, when told 'I understand' will respond by saying 'No you bloody don't!'

2 **Encourage them to talk**. Ask open questions (ones that start 'how', 'what' or 'why' and therefore beg full answers). The word 'why?', especially used on its own, can seem rather blunt, or even pushy. It can be better to ask 'What's the reason for that ...?' or 'What makes you think that?' It's also important to get the person to talk about their emotions; it's usually the emotions that cause the problems at work, after all. Peter's lateness may have a practical cause, but his change in behaviour is an emotional problem. So ask him questions about how he feels. At this stage you are simply gathering information – don't start volunteering your own comments. Just keep asking questions.

Your body language can also be used to encourage people to talk:

- let them see that your attention is focused on them
- make eye contact
- make listening noises
- sit in a relaxed posture
- lean forward slightly – it indicates full attention.

Encourage them by summarising their key comments: 'So the problem in the mornings is that you've had to take over doing the school run twice a week?'

The one thing you can do, apart from asking questions, that will help the other person to relax, is to admit your own weaknesses. People hate opening up, especially to the 'boss', because they think they will be seen as weak and unable to cope. So let them know that they're not alone. Find opportunities to say 'I'm always making that mistake' or 'yes, that's one of my weaknesses too'. Once again, don't be untruthful – but don't miss an opportunity to verbalise the truth.

There's one other point about encouraging people to talk – don't judge. This will shut people up faster than anything. Whatever private opinion you may have, don't let them see it. No one likes being judged, and they won't put themselves in line for it; they'll just clam up. If it turns out that Peter's partner left because Peter had a string of affairs, don't say: 'Well you've only yourself to blame really then, haven't you?' Remember your own objective – to help resolve Peter's problem so that his performance will return to its previous level and the morale of the team won't be damaged. Passing judgement on him is not going to help you reach that objective.

3 **Examine the options**. Once you feel you have gathered all the relevant information you can, and Peter's got his feelings off his chest, you need to guide him onto this stage of the conversation. There isn't a fixed length of time a counselling session should take, but it will normally be between half an hour and an hour. If it goes on longer than this, it's probably become rambling and non-directional somewhere in the middle. So after about 15 to 30 minutes you should start to feel the time is right to move onto this stage.

This is not, repeat *not*, about giving advice. We'll examine the reasons for that when we come to look at how to find a solution. At this stage, the idea is to be totally neutral. You want to throw every option into the ring and you want Peter to suggest as many of them as possible. It's his problem after all.

Start by saying something along the lines of 'So how do you see the options?' or 'What do you think would help resolve the problem?' You can throw in the odd helpful comment, but don't attach any opinions to it. Don't give Peter any idea as to whether you think it's a good idea or a bad idea. It's just an option. For example: 'You could arrive half an hour later until the problem is sorted, in exchange for cutting your lunch break or staying half an hour later at the end of the day.' You're not expressing a view, you're simply stating a fact. You might privately think it would be better if Peter employed a nanny who could drive, or gave up his affair and tried to persuade his partner to return.

By the end of this stage of the counselling session, you should have as broad a range of options as possible on the table. Most of the options that involve Peter's home situation will have been offered by Peter ('I could ask the school to find more parents to share the school run with'). You should, in particular, have offered options based on information that Peter may not have known: 'We have a staff counselling service here which I could refer you to'.

Finding a solution

The key to finding a solution is to let the person with the problem find it. If they feel pressured into a solution they aren't happy with it's less likely to work. Not only that, but it's important to accept that they 'own' the problem. It's theirs. That means that it's their responsibility to find a solution to it – no one has the right to take it out of their hands. When someone is under stress and vulnerable they find it harder to say 'no', and it's far easier than you might think to pressure them unwittingly into adopting your preferred solution, if you let them find out what it is.

When you give someone advice, you are effectively offering to take over the problem. They give you their problem (which they own) and you solve it for them. That means you have responsibility for both the problem and the solution. And when it doesn't work it's down to you. The other person has no vested interest in your solution working – because you took over responsibility for it. Part of the problem is that in a counselling situation, people will probably be polite and accept your solution, even if they don't like it. And don't forget that as far as they are concerned 'you're the boss' which makes it even harder to disagree with you.

It should go without saying, therefore, that once they have decided which solution they are going to go for, you must agree to it without argument. You'll have discounted any non-options at the previous stage: 'I'm afraid we can't give you six months paid leave' – so all the choices left are valid options. So support their solution and agree a course of action with them. For example, if Peter wants to come in later for a few weeks, agree how many weeks he needs the arrangement to stand for and set a date to review the situation shortly before this time limit expires.

Finally, as you conclude the counselling session, make it clear that if Peter wants to talk again any time – about this problem, new developments or any other problem – your door is open.

Counselling dos and don'ts

To summarise, here are the key points for counselling members of your team with personal problems that are affecting their work:

1. **Set the scene**. Make sure it is:
   - private
   - uninterrupted
   - relaxed.
2. **Discuss the problem**. Acknowledge the person's feelings:
   - reassure them that their response is valid
   - boost their self-respect.

   Encourage them to talk:
   - ask open questions
   - show you're listening
   - summarise key remarks
   - admit your own weaknesses.

   Examine the options:

- place all the options on the table
- offer only facts, not opinions
- provide information about options that the other person doesn't know.

3 **Find a solution**. Let the person with the problem find the solution.

- support their decision
- agree a course of action
- set a review date
- let them know the door is always open.

And here are a few counselling pitfalls to avoid:

- **Don't** try to fill every silence.
- **Don't** say 'I understand'.
- **Don't** judge.
- **Don't** give advice.

Coping with stress

Certain kinds of stress are perfectly healthy; you could call this positive stress. Some people work better under pressure – it lends an excitement to work. If everything is easy, there are no challenges and no deadlines, and things can get very boring. But there is also negative stress – too much pressure – which can be counter-productive, unhealthy and even dangerous. An estimated 1.7 million working days are lost every year in England and Wales alone due to work-related stress. And of course in extreme cases stress can lead to serious illness including heart disease. So it's clearly important to make sure that none of your team are suffering.

Recognising the signs

The symptoms of stress vary according to the degree of it. Early warning signs to watch out for include:

- taking work home regularly
- failing to take holidays.

The people who suffer these particular symptoms tend to drive themselves to achieve more and better all the time. They often start out enjoying the pressure they put themselves under. But it generally gets on top of them sooner or later, and they find it hard to ease off because their productivity will obviously drop if they go back to working an eight hour day. What they often fail to realise is that eventually their productivity will drop anyway as a result of mounting stress.

If things progress unchecked, other signs can emerge:

- tiredness
- irritability
- criticising other people
- carrying out tasks in a panicky or flappy manner
- poor concentration
- poor memory
- complaining of headaches or back pain.

Obviously some people are naturally more critical or irritable than others. So, as with personal problems that interfere with work, the thing to look out for is any change in behaviour.

Eventually, in the serious stages, the signs you should notice include:

- exhaustion
- apathy
- lack of commitment
- lack of enjoyment in their work
- a tendency to catch every bug going round
- sudden outbursts of emotion or shaking.

Identifying the causes

Once you have established that someone on your team is stressed, you need to try to work out why. It helps if you can do this before you talk to them about it (it will only take you a few minutes to sit down and think it through), because it will be helpful to consider solutions that are in your power rather than theirs to apply, before you sit down and discuss it with them.

Here are the most common causes of stress at work; go through them and see which you think might apply:

- too many deadlines, or deadlines that are too tight
- frequent interruptions making it impossible to get anything done
- poor performance
- long hours
- workload too heavy
- poor prioritising
- isolated working conditions
- bad working relationships
- insecurity/fear of redundancy
- internal conflict (work vs home, or employer's demands vs professional standards).

These are the most common causes of work-related stress, but obviously the list is not complete. There may be conditions that are peculiar to your team that are contributing to stress among its members so you need to consider these as well.

You should find as you work through the list that you can narrow down the causes of stress in the team member you are concerned about, and may well be able to identify the solution quite easily.

Finding the solutions

Stress affects people similarly to the kind of personal problems that we have just looked at, so it's hardly surprising that it needs to be handled in a similar fashion. Not only that, but it may actually *be* one of those personal problems. If you can't find a ready explanation for someone's stressed behaviour, it may be that the cause is not work-related. They could be going through a stressful situation of some kind in their personal life.

So the approach to take is to set up a counselling session, following the guidelines outlined in this chapter. If the person agrees that their stress is work-related, ask them to tell you what they think the cause is before you give them your opinion. If they are unsure, or you're not convinced that they have identified the full reason behind it, offer your opinion – and note the word 'offer'. Don't say 'Let me tell you what I think …', say 'Do you think it's possible that it might be caused by …?'

Once you have agreed on the cause of the problem, you need to find a solution. This differs slightly from counselling people through personal problems, because you have identified a practical problem rather than an emotional one, and can therefore find a practical solution. However the practical problem does have emotional effects which you musn't ignore completely.

In effect, you must still have the person's support for any solution or it may not work. But the likelihood is that if you simply promise to remove the cause of the stress they'll feel instantly happier and their performance will improve along with their health. Unfortunately though, there is a slight hitch. It's not always that easy to remove the cause of the stress. But it's generally possible to ameliorate this in some way. The table below goes through the stress factors we listed earlier, and suggests a few solutions to them.

Stress factor	Solution
Deadlines	Have a look at their workload and see whether the deadlines are unreasonable. If they are, change the schedules or remove some of the workload. If you feel they are not unreasonable, talk it through with them. You could set interim deadlines so the person can never get too far behind: instead of saying 'I want this report on Friday week' say 'I'd like the outline for this report next Wednesday, and the first draft the following Tuesday. Then I'd like the finished document on Friday week.' It may also help to give the person some time management training.
Interruptions	Talk through the various methods of minimising interruptions; they may not know the tricks of the trade. If they are underassertive they may find it hard to say 'not now' to people. Assertiveness or time management training may help. If their desk is open to the rest of the team, perhaps you could site them somewhere less likely to be disturbed. Or allow them to use a meeting room or spare office for an hour or two when they're working on something that takes a lot of concentration.
Poor performance	If someone is stressed by this, they clearly care, and will be doing their best to remedy it. It's likely, therefore, that they cannot help falling short of their targets. In this case see if you can identify the problem area (such as poor time management, or too heavy a workload). Training may help, or it may be that you need to reduce their workload or adjust their targets to a more practical and achievable level.

Stress Factor	Solution
Long hours	People who take work home are either trying to impress you or they have too much work. If they are trying to impress, let them know that they don't have to. Make it clear that you judge your team members' ability on what they can achieve during working hours. If they genuinely have too much work, do something about relieving the load.
Workload too heavy	Again, this could be poor time management, in which case training can help, or it may be that the workload really is too heavy, in which case you'll need to reduce it.
Poor prioritising	Discuss the problems of prioritising, and establish why they find it difficult. Give them training if necessary, and perhaps ask them to spend five minutes with you every Monday morning for a few weeks to go through their priorities with you.
Isolated working conditions	Some people love to work alone, but for some it is a real stress provoker; they need human contact. Find a way for these people to spend more time around others, or perhaps take them out of a lone office and put them in an open-plan office (which is better for building team spirit anyway, as we've already seen).
Bad working relationships	Specific situations are dealt with elsewhere in the book, but if there is a persistent problem try to minimise contact between the people who don't get on – make sure they don't have to sit at neighbouring desks, for example – and follow the general guidelines at the end of Chapter 1.
Insecurity/fear of redundancy	Reassure these people if you can. Occasionally however, there is a real threat of redundancy or relocation. You can't change the facts, but these people's stress will be minimised if you keep them as fully informed as possible. Tell them what you can, and tell them when you'll know more. Keep them posted.
Internal conflict	Sometimes you can help people prioritise, or you can argue on their behalf in the organisation. Suppose someone is expected to organise ten major presentations a month. They can do it, but they know they could do it better if they were less pressured. They are stressed by

knowing their performance is below par, and being unable to improve it wouthout reducing the workoad. Your assistance or support in arguing for an assistant, for example, can help. Sometimes these stresses can't be resolved though; if the cause is a high-powered job that conflicts with their home life, you may be able to help a little but ultimately they may have to choose between the job and their family.

Some problems aren't going to go away because they are caused by trying to fit a square peg into a round hole. In other words, some people become frustrated and stressed because they are unsuited to the job they are being asked to do. This may not be anything to do with skills or abilities; it could be a matter of personality. One or two of the stress factors listed above are sometimes a result of this, such as bad working relationships. In this case have a look at the personality types described in Chapter 1, and the solutions listed there to dealing with people who aren't suited to the roles they are in.

If you feel that someone is in an advanced state of stress you will need to suggest more drastic measures. You may even have to insist – kindly but firmly – for the sake of their own health. If you have a company counsellor or doctor you could refer them there. Otherwise try to persuade them to seek professional help themselves. If the symptoms are serious enough it may even be wise to suggest they take time off, or advise them strongly to take the holiday entitlement they haven't been using. Generally speaking, however, you will have recognised the symptoms long before they reach this stage. You'll have recognised the signs, identified the causes and found the solution.

Creating a culture that reduces people problems

Any individual problem quickly becomes a team problem, like it or not, as its psychological effect on the individual spreads to the rest of the group. So you need to identify personal and stress-related problems quickly, and deal with them for everyone's sake.

You can't stop people having problems. The single most important thing you *can* do is to make sure that you find out about any problems as soon as possible, and encourage people to talk to you and let you help them. The best way to do that is to be approachable and react in a positive, encouraging, helpful way whenever problems do arise. It won't take long before people start to feel comfortable about coming to you before you've had a chance to approach them. They'll think 'That talk we had last time I had problems was much easier than I'd expected – and it certainly helped.' And team members will tell each other that it's worth going to you when they have problems.

A few final points:

1 **Follow up the counselling session informally**. Not only with a review session, but also show your concern by asking the person how they are getting on – in private, if they haven't told everyone their problems. It doesn't have to be a formal session – ask them at the end of a meeting when there are only the two of you there. Don't overdo it and ask them every other day, but the occasional 'Are things improving at home?' or 'How are you coping with the kids now?' shows that you care. It also gives them an opportunity to talk if things have deteriorated again: 'Well, actually, I could do with another chat sometime...'.

2 **Never break a confidence**. If any one in your team discovers that you've ever passed on information that was given confidentially at a counselling session, you'll be lucky if any of them ever discusses their problems with you again – which deprives you of the opportunity to help resolve things for the benefit of the individual and the team.

3 **Stick to your word**. If you tell someone that taking a certain course of action won't count against them, make sure it doesn't. If a stressed team member is worried about losing productivity if they stop taking work home with them, and you tell them that it's all right, you're not asking them to be superhuman, don't tell them at their next appraisal that you want to discuss their drop in productivity. Your team members need to trust you before they will confide in you.

So you see, dealing with people's problems really isn't that hard. It's just a matter of forgetting that you're supposed to be the boss, and addressing their problems in a similar way to the way you would address anyone else's outside the workplace. Listen, sympathise and don't give advice, and you can't go far wrong.

CHAPTER FOUR

Problem people

We may like to be positive and see the best in everyone, but there's no denying that some members of a team are easier to work with than others. This chapter is about how to work with difficult people; people who are difficult because of their personalities, not because of a lack of skills or knowledge. Chapter 6 will deal with interviewing skills including appraisal and discipline interviews, so in this chapter we will look at the sort of problems that don't – or at least don't yet – warrant a formal approach. The real reason for addressing them is not that you personally find these traits irritating, it is that the team as a whole will function better if it doesn't have someone in its midst who is frustrating or difficult for the others to work with.

In the Introduction we saw how important it is to remember that you can't change people's personalities, but you can encourage them to change their behaviour. The techniques in this chapter are all based on that premise. The important thing is to find ways to build on people's positive qualities and minimise the effects of their negative traits.

One of the key techniques for handling problem people is known as feedback. This chapter starts with a look at how to use feedback, and then gives a kind of 'troubleshooter's guide' to using feedback and other techniques to handle over 20 of the most common types of problem people.

Feedback

We're all guilty of it sometimes: someone irritates us and we bite our tongue, we bottle up our feelings, we give no clue that we don't like their behaviour and then, finally, we snap. Either we grind the other person down and make them feel small, or they retaliate and we end up having a row. And we were only trying to be tolerant.

We really aren't being fair to the other person a lot of the time. They can't help the way they are – least of all if no one tells them it's a problem. Maybe they find us just as irritating in other ways. Feedback is about addressing our differences with other people in a non-confrontational way. This means it's not such an unpleasant way to approach someone, so you don't have to wait until you're at breaking point before you do it.

Personality problems are difficult to deal with. There's nothing in the job description that says a person is not allowed to adopt a negative attitude, or to complain if they're not satisfied with things. So it's not necessarily a matter for formal procedures. On the other hand, as leader you may see your team becoming disunited through personality clashes, and it's your job to prevent it. (The next chapter looks in more detail at conflict between team members.) So you have to do something.

It simply isn't reasonable or productive to call someone in and say 'The whole team finds you difficult to work with'. They will feel you've all been discussing them behind their back and they will be highly embarrassed, or very angry. These matters are personal and must be dealt with one-to-one. If the whole team feels the same way then everyone in the team should speak to the person individually. However as leader, you need to be the first to tackle the problem. With any luck this will save the rest of the team from having to tackle it at all, and save the person involved the embarrassment of effectively having to deal with the issue in front of everyone.

The principles of feedback are very simple, and can be applied to any personality problem (as well as a lot of work-based problems):

1. Obviously you need to speak to the person in private, and at a time when neither of you is in a particular rush.
2. Decide in advance what the key points you want to make are, and prepare ways of saying them that do not include:
   - exaggeration, such as 'you're always complaining'

- judgements, such as 'you're hopeless at dealing with problems yourself'
- labels, such as 'you're a whinger'.

3 When you speak to the person, focus on yourself and not them. Don't start sentences with 'You make me feel...', try saying 'I feel...when you...'. For example 'I feel helpless and frustrated when you complain about things that I feel are minor details.'

4 Explain why you feel this way: 'I can't deal with them myself because I have other claims on my time which take higher priority; but I feel helpless having to say no to you.'

5 Now let the other person have their say. Listen to them, and show you're listening.

6 Focus on how they *behave*, not what they (in your view) *are*.

7 Be prepared to quote actual instances wherever possible.

8 Relate their behaviour to the task: point out how they are impairing the team's ability to get results.

9 Be positive as well. Tell them when they have done well by not arguing, complaining or whatever. Show them they *can* behave co-operatively.

10 Suggest a solution and see how the other person feels. This is very important; as we saw in the Introduction you can't change people's personalities, only their behaviour. So you must have an alternative behaviour in your mind that you are asking them to adopt – if you can't think of any solutions, you'd be better off not tackling the matter in the first place. Remember, you're not asking them to stop being a complaining person – they can't do that – you're asking them (perhaps not in so many words) to be a complainer who doesn't complain about certain things or at certain times. For example: 'Could you suggest a solution when you explain the problem to me? Try to think of something that doesn't involve time or resources that aren't available. Then when you talk to me I'll be better able to help and you'll find the complaint is more likely to be dealt with effectively.'

11 Listen to the other person's response and be prepared to compromise with them. (You may even learn something about how *you* appear to them, and be able to adapt your own behaviour and improve your performance.)

You'll find that many of the difficult personality traits listed below can be dealt with without even having to discuss them with the person directly. But if the characteristic is very strongly marked, and the person doesn't respond to the techniques listed below, use feedback.

The problem people

The uncommunicative person

Some people are naturally slow to contribute to conversations and may genuinely not realise how unhelpful they are being. One of the problems associated with this behaviour is that these people often fail to commit themselves to anything because they tend to speak in 'Mmms' and 'Uh-huhs' rather than using phrases such as 'I'll have it ready by Tuesday morning'. Consequently they often infuriate their fellow team members who feel they can't rely on them. Feedback is often very effective, but before you try it, here are a few tips that may ease the situation:

- ask these people a lot of questions to encourage them to talk, and make the questions as specific as you can. So don't ask 'Can you get this report done next week?' but 'This report needs to be about 5,000 words, and I need it on Thursday week at the latest. Will you be able to do that?';
- except when eliciting commitments from them, ask open questions (ones to which they cannot reply 'yes' or 'no'). This forces them to communicate more;
- once you've asked a question, shut up and wait for them to answer. Don't feel uncomfortable – the onus is on them to speak first so tough it out;
- don't expect to convert these people into being good communicators; you won't. Just encourage them to communicate enough for the rest of the team to be able to work with them comfortably.

The person who never listens

These people can be incredibly frustrating for everyone. Not only do you know damn well they're not really listening while you're speaking to them, but tasks frequently don't get done as a result. And when you tackle them they claim you never told them about it in the first place. There is, however, a simple technique for dealing with this:

- when you've finished speaking, say: 'I want to be certain I'm making this clear. Could you just repeat it back to me?';

- if you are worried they're repeating back to you parrot fashion and still won't remember, ask them questions – open ones, so they can't just say 'mmm': 'What do you think about including case studies in the report, and how should we work them in if we use them?';
- these people will never remember what you did over the weekend – just concentrate on making sure they remember what they need in order to get the job done well.

The daydreamer

The problem with daydreamers is that their productivity drops when they start to dream, and they tend to make mistakes. As a result they often let down their colleagues on the team. The chief cause tends to be boredom, so the best treatment is to keep their attention going:

- give them tasks to share with someone else – the other person will keep them awake and on their toes;
- as far as possible, let them decide which tasks they want to do when;
- set them productivity targets paired with accuracy targets, and with good incentives for meeting them;
- accept that these people will never be suited to certain kinds of monotonous work and try to avoid giving such work to them.

The loner

Loners are happy that way. They like keeping their office door shut. The problem with having them on the team is that they aren't really team players. As a result they can appear quite remote and often negative to the rest of the team, and can inhibit a free flow of ideas. Here are some suggestions:

- loners tend to withdraw further if they are put under pressure to be social. As we've established by now you can't change them, so you might as well accommodate them. In fact, this will probably improve matters. Allow them their privacy and don't force them to attend large gatherings;
- loners are often more comfortable talking to people on the phone than face-to-face.

So call them on the internal phone sometimes instead of walking round to their office;

- recognise that these people have certain positive qualities: they tend to work well on their own, have a bent for detailed work, and can be very good at working on long-term projects. Exploit these talents, and make sure the rest of the team members appreciate them also – they may well be glad to pass these tasks on to someone who wants to do them.

The secretive person

Some people make a habit of keeping back information from the rest of the team, which makes it impossible for everyone to feel that they're pulling together. It helps to understand why people do this. There are two common reasons for it: one is that it gives them a feeling of power, and the other is that they have a particularly strong need for recognition. Here are some suggestions for dealing with such people:

- make your requests for information very specific, and put them in writing if necessary;
- alternatively, write down the information you already have and ask them to fill in the blanks for you; this should satisfy any need for power that they have. They'll get a feeling of satisfaction from being able to tell you what you didn't know;
- when they give you the information you wanted, be warm and generous with your thanks so they feel smart for having been able to supply it. Do this in front of other people when you can. This should satisfy their need to have their contribution acknowledged;
- you should be able to tell from their reaction to these approaches which of the two reasons for being secretive applies in your case. Once you've worked out which of the approaches suits them best you can concentrate on that. In future you should have no problems getting information out of them.

The sulker

People sulk because they want to let you know how upset they are. If they didn't sulk (they feel) you would think the matter wasn't important to them. Almost all of us are prone to sulk occasionally, but some people do it over such seemingly minor issues that it ends up happening frequently and creates an unpleasant and unhelpful attitude that can permeate the whole team. Remember:

- sulking is intended to make you feel guilty once you realise how upset the person is. Any approach to handling a sulker only works if you honestly have nothing to feel guilty about. So when you have the kind of discussion with this person that can lead to the sulks, make sure you genuinely listen to them with an open mind, explain the reasons behind your view of the matter, and act in a friendly and reasonable way. Once the discussion is over, if they choose to sulk you know that there is nothing else you could have done except give in for no good reason, simply to avoid the sulks;
- the aim is that you will capitulate. Never, ever do so. If it works for them once, they will try it every time;
- don't perpetuate the atmosphere by being short with them either. Behave as if everything were normal. If they give you the silent treatment, just say 'OK, we'll sort it out later.' If it really can't wait, force them to answer you. Ask them the question and then wait for their response. And wait...and wait. Force them to break the silence by answering – it's their turn to speak after all. Once you've shown them that you can hold out longer than them, they won't try that technique again;
- remember that most of us sulk to some extent over major issues when we think our feelings aren't being taken seriously. Even frequent sulkers occasionally have a genuine case – they really aren't being listened to or considered over something important. So always make a mental check when they get upset and satisfy yourself that this isn't one of those occasions – or if it is, hear them out.

The over-sensitive person

Every tiny criticism is taken as a personal slight with these people, making it almost impossible to discuss their work objectively. You'll always have to watch what you say, but there are ways to minimise the problem:

- never make any comment they could take offence at in front of other people; this will make them feel humiliated;
- make sure that your criticisms are objective, specific and worded so as to be clearly criticisms of their work and not themselves. So don't say 'I'm a bit worried about

your performance lately' say 'I'm a bit worried that you've missed two deadlines in the last month';

- build their self-confidence. Always point out where they have done well when you discuss their weak points: 'Mind you, although you delivered the work a day late, it was a terrific report.' Comment on strengths of personality as well as work: 'You have a real knack for seeing to the heart of an issue';
- remember that since these people are so sensitive, a little criticism goes a long way. If you say 'I'm a bit worried' they'll feel they've turned in the worst month's work in history. If you say 'I'm not satisfied with this report' they'll be heading for the razor blades before you've finished the sentence. So go easy on them.

The martyr

Martyrs are always taking on extra work, and moaning about it. 'Still, someone's got to do it...go on, I'll add it to my in-tray...don't worry, I'll manage...'. The problem with martyrs is that they often make other people feel guilty for not working as hard as them, and their tension and negativity can spread through the team. They are also very prone to stress (which we dealt with in the last chapter).

You can't convert a martyr into a laid back, relaxed person. But you can minimise the disruption they cause around them:

- don't allow them to take on extra work. Keep their workload to a reasonable level and politely decline any offers to help out with urgent or extra tasks. Encourage them to take full lunch breaks and to go home on time;
- if necessary, have a private talk to tell them you're concerned about the stress they put themselves under. Make it clear to them that you don't expect them to take on extra work, and you won't think them any less able if they keep their workload down;
- you could tactfully point out that their effect on the rest of the team is counter-productive. Bear in mind however that martyrs are often extremely sensitive so be very diplomatic. You could imply, for example, that others are inclined to feel inferior because they don't have the martyr's stamina, and that this damages morale;
- martyrs often feel inadequate themselves and are driven by a need to prove their ability and boost their self-confidence. So make sure you give them plenty of recog-

nition for the work they do. Reduce this slightly when they overwork, and shift it to concern for their health and the team's morale. They are more likely to prefer the response they get when they work less hard.

The moaner

There are two good points worth making about people who constantly complain (honest):

1. they will often be the ones who bring genuine problems to your attention; problems that you want to know about. Because of their natural tendency to moan, the team will often unofficially appoint them as spokesperson for the group, and when they come to you they may be airing a commonly held complaint.
2. they are often very conscientious workers. If they weren't, they wouldn't care when things went wrong. It's because they care that they complain.

   Bear these points in mind when a team member comes to you with their latest complaint. The following will minimise the minor whinges they come to you with:

- don't make decisions that affect them directly without consulting them first. If they feel involved in any changes or new procedures they will feel less inclined to moan;
- try to avoid putting them under pressure – this almost always causes this kind of person to complain;
- *Before* they complain, ask them if they need any help. Occasionally they may see this as an invitation to complain, but more often than not they will tell you things are fine (if they'd thought of a complaint they'd have voiced it already). Once they have committed themselves to the attitude that everything's OK it makes it harder for them to start moaning later;
- when they do complain, these people are prone to keep analysing the reasons why the problem has arisen. Focus them on the solution instead. 'Well, it's happened now. What do you think is the best way to resolve it?' Just occasionally it may be useful to know the background so you can prevent the problem recurring, but even so, suggest to them: 'Let's identify the reason for the situation later; for now, let's just worry about resolving it.'

The pessimist

When someone says 'It'll never work' it's extremely frustrating as well as being unconstructive. On the other hand, the pessimists are often the ones who stop the team from making mistakes. But they need careful handling to exploit their ability to spot flaws, and stop them dragging the team down:

- when they express a negative view, ask them to make it specific: Why won't it work? Are they guessing or are they basing their assessment on the facts? Is it just a hunch or do they have previous experience of this sort of thing? Be firm about getting them to be precise about which part of the project will create difficulties and why;
- ask them how they think the problem can be resolved. Again, get them to be specific; don't settle for 'I don't know – the whole thing looks like a waste of time to me';
- pessimists are often afraid of failure, and therefore avoid taking risks. They try to stop the whole team taking risks as well, by adopting such a negative viewpoint. Try asking them to tell you what they think the worst possible scenario could be as a result of following the course of action under discussion. This process often helps them to get their feelings in perspective;
- remove their fear of failure by relieving them of as much responsibility as possible. Then even if the project does fail, it won't be *their* failure. Either tell them you will take responsibility for the decision, or make it clear that the team as a whole is responsible (which dilutes their personal ownership of the project). Often, with this burden lifted, pessimists can become helpful contributors – although they will never become optimists.

The prejudiced person

There are all sorts of prejudice you can encounter at work. The most commonly cited are sexism and racism, but some people dislike working for people younger than them, or sharing an office with someone from a different social background. You haven't a hope of persuading someone through reasoned argument to change this kind of attitude. Often the best way to resolve this kind of problem is the feedback approach outlined at the beginning of the chapter. But it is sometimes possible to change these people's behaviour without broaching the subject directly. For example:

- don't get into arguments about whether women are as good as men, whether experience is everything, whether the immigration laws are too lenient or whether all people educated at public school are snobs. Just remember, *you* have as much chance of convincing them of your point of view as *they* have of persuading you round to their way of thinking;

- *show* them they're wrong. Let's take sexism as an example. If you have a sexist man on your team make sure that the women on the team have the chance to demonstrate that their abilities aren't restricted by their sex. Give them traditionally male tasks to do. Once their sexist colleague sees they can do them perfectly well, their attitude may soften;
- make sure you don't inadvertently reinforce their prejudice – you might want to talk about this to other team members who are affected. For instance, a woman who asks a sexist man to change the light bulb in her office is reinforcing his prejudice. It may be that she's only asking because she's not tall enough to reach it herself, but she still isn't doing her cause any good. Far better to stand on a chair and change the bulb herself, or at least wait until he's out of the office and then ask someone else.

The jobsworth type

The jobsworth won't do anything that isn't down in black and white in their job description. These people can crush team spirit. Forget co-operation, forget mutual support – they're not interested. You need to find out why if you can. Often, jobsworths behave as they do because they feel unappreciated. If you thank them generously when they do you a favour they'll be more inclined to put themselves out for you next time. So how do you get them to do you the first favour?

- you need to appreciate, as they already do, that if it's not on their job description they don't have to do it. It's no good getting annoyed or frustrated. They're absolutely entitled to say no;
- they know the rule book and their own job description like the back of their hand, so you'd better know it too. Then at least you'll know whether you're asking them to do something they're paid to do, or whether you're asking them a favour;
- if you're asking them to do something outside their remit, let them know that you know that you're asking a favour. Don't say 'Please get today's orders over to despatch', say 'I know you're busy but Kim's off sick and today's orders need to go over to despatch. Would you mind taking them?'

- if they say no, accept it gracefully. If you say 'That's fair enough, it's not your job' you're showing them that you respect their rights. This approach might at least soften them up for next time;
- if you want them to do you favours make it a two-way deal, and thank and reward them for it.
- encourage co-operation between all members of your team. The jobsworth may learn from the others' example, and they may sometimes be more easily persuaded by other members of the team than by you;
- jobsworths sometimes behave as they do because they suffer from a deep insecurity and fear of the repercussions that will result if they make a mistake. It is therefore important that you don't bawl them out if they do slip up.

The control freak

These people are so nervous of being let down that they find it virtually impossible to delegate or share work. This both frustrates and excludes their colleagues. They are often perfectionists and they need recognition – that's why they find being let down so painful. Control freaks cannot change their innate fear of being let down, but they can learn – in the right circumstances – to change their behaviour and delegate more work to others. The following points are worth noting:

- these people are happy if they know they can trust people to work to as high a standard as they do. So allow them to delegate or share work at a more gradual rate than most people, so they can learn one step at a time that the people around them can be trusted;
- while they are learning this, encourage people to keep them posted as to what is going on, and ask their advice where necessary. This way they are continually aware that the task is being carried out satisfactorily;
- if anyone around them makes a mistake, let them see that it's an opportunity to learn and the mistake won't be repeated. Encourage people to admit their mistakes and actively demonstrate that they have learnt from them (this is a good general practice anyway): 'I arranged the meeting over a month ago and wrote it in the diary, but I never called back to confirm because the arrangement had been definite. I hadn't thought that the customer might change their schedule and forget to tell me. Still,

after wasting an hour and a half travelling to see someone who wasn't there, that's one mistake I shan't make again. I'm going to confirm every appointment I ever make from now on.' This kind of self-assessment will give the control freak confidence that the lesson really has sunk in;

- as team leader, you can sit these people down and ask them what the worst possible scenario is if someone does mess up. Often it's not really that bad, and getting them to verbalise it helps them to see it in perspective;
- if you have people on the team who are prone to make the kind of mistakes the control freak hates, don't invite trouble by asking them to work closely together;
- once a control freak has learnt to trust someone, you should find that they become excellent at delegating – at least to that person – and they'll be more open-minded about learning to trust someone else after a happy experience last time. So try to put them together with one of the most reliable team members while you're unofficially training them to trust their colleagues more.

The know-all

Know-alls are infuriating. You find yourself wanting them to be wrong even though the project and the team will suffer – and that's not healthy. But how do you stop them frustrating everyone?

- know-alls tend to knock people's confidence by crediting themselves with every good idea and every success. So for a start you can keep everyone else's confidence boosted – particularly those who work closely with the know-all;
- know-alls are incapable of saying 'I was wrong'. Rather than pointing out their errors to them, ask them to explain their ideas or plans to you so that they can spot their own mistakes as they speak. If they don't identify them, ask them questions that focus on the area you feel needs closer examination;
- don't try to humiliate them in front of other people, tempting though it may be – you will only antagonise them;
- give them credit where it's due, but make them share it: 'That was a very good idea, Pat. Mind you, we'd never have got the results we did from it without Jason's inspired planning. And Jacky's presentation was first class.' Make sure the know-all recognises everyone else's contribution as well as their own.

The prima donna

It's no coincidence that these people are prone to act like five year olds. This kind of behaviour is usually learned in early childhood; they discover that by creating a scene they can get what they want. In a team environment, however, you want people to focus on what is the best way to achieve the team's objectives, not on fulfilling their personal agenda:

- the prima donna has learnt that this kind of behaviour gets them what they want. All you have to do is to teach them that it doesn't – at least not here. It may take time after years of finding it successful, but if you're consistent they'll learn in the end;
- don't respond to this kind of behaviour. Find an excuse to leave the room – to make a phone call or grab a coffee – and come back when they've calmed down. Be responsive and willing to listen as soon as they're calm and rational, but opt out of the conversation whenever they become childish;
- don't meet their emotion with emotion of your own: meet it with cool, objective, factual statements and questions.

The rowdy person

They sing to themselves while they're waiting for the phone to be answered, they burp loudly, they laugh uproariously at things they're reading to themselves – in short, they're cheerful, jolly and well meaning, and their colleagues are frustrated, irritable and underproductive. Here are some suggestions:

- it can help to have an informal word with these people. They generally have no idea that they are disrupting everyone; often they think they're being helpful in keeping everyone's spirits up. So be positive in your approach: 'It's great to have someone cheerful and optimistic around, especially when things start to get a bit pressured. The only trouble is …';
- if the problem doesn't diminish after this, the best solution can be to put physical distance between this person and the rest of the team. Put them in the corner of an open-plan office, or give them their own room if you have individual offices. It might be more tactful to give a different explanation for doing this. Instead of squashing their zest for life by saying 'No one wants to sit near you' you could say 'It makes

sense for you to be nearer the fax machine' or 'you meet a lot of customers at the offices – you really need your own room';

- you can't change these people's natural ebullience, and you really shouldn't try. There are times when it is exactly what the team needs. For example, these people often keep everyone's spirits up in a crisis.

The over-competitive person

Team members competing with each other can work well if it's done on a friendly level, and especially if there's an element of luck involved – such as who happens to answer the phone to the customer placing the huge order. It can spur people on and help keep them motivated. But over-competitiveness can be very destructive, as well as being demoralising to anyone who can't keep up and so always 'loses'. The following points are worth bearing in mind:

- concentrate on focusing the team's performance on its customers (whether they are internal or external), not on each other. Explain to the team collectively (in a friendly, informal way) that you'd like them to channel their competitive drive outwards rather than inwards;
- if an over-competitive person can't ease up, try to encourage them to compete against themselves, and beat their own targets;
- occasionally someone takes competitiveness so seriously that they start to keep back information from other members of the team in order to give themselves a competitive advantage over them. This does the team immeasurable damage and you will have to speak directly to the person about it explaining why it is bad for the team;
- a few people are born so competitively-natured that they just can't help it. If nothing else works, your best option might be to allocate them tasks where they work independently and therefore have nothing to compete over.

The domineering person

Bullying within the team destroys any chance of real team spirit, and it needs to be controlled. Of course you can't eradicate it completely. That's all right; you don't need to. You just need to reduce it to a level where the rest of the team can handle it:

- domineering people often pick on the weakest person around – often the youngest, least experienced member of the team. Stand up for this person until they learn to stand up for themselves. Don't be aggressive in their defence, or confrontational, but don't allow the domineering person to bully them. If they are trying to dragoon them into doing an urgent task which they don't have time for, come to their support and say: 'Actually, Peter has got his priorities right. The research he's doing for Jacky is very urgent and he can't do anything else until he's completed that';
- domineering people tend to try and shout other people down. Don't react. If everyone else stays calm they will start to look rather silly losing their cool. They'll soon learn to stay in control rather than make a fool of themselves.

The aggressive type

This type of person can upset other team members. Aggressive people tend to think and act fast, and they are often insecure and need recognition and personal power. These aspects of their make-up can guide you in dealing with them:

- because they like to get on with things, it eases your relationship with them if you can move at their speed on projects you're working closely with them on;
- they need recognition and will sometimes put people down in order to make themselves appear superior. If you give them credit when they deserve it they won't need to do this;
- aggressive people don't necessarily want you to capitulate to them all the time – they often don't like people who are wet. They would much rather be able to respect you. So stand up to them firmly (but non-aggressively) when you need to.

The manipulator

Good manipulators never leave any evidence; you can't actually *prove* that they've been manipulative. But you know it anyway. And so does everyone else. There's no point challenging them directly because they'll deny it. So make them feel that you want to help, not to point the finger:

- if they are manipulating a situation, they must have a reason. Think it through and work out what they are trying to achieve;

- talk to them without accusing them of manipulation: 'I get the feeling that you'd like to run the ABC Ltd account. Is that right?';
- they will probably agree with you, but if they deny it give them reasons why you have this impression. 'I noticed at the meeting last Thursday that you highlighted one or two errors that Pat had made recently with the account. You don't normally focus on that kind of detail unless you have a particular interest in the subject – so I concluded that you were probably interested in the ABC account';
- once the manipulator feels they can talk confidentially and openly to you, without fear of accusations of manipulation, they will do so. After all, they are more likely to achieve their aim that way;
- if you can't give them what they want, explain the reasons to them. 'Pat is running the account well, albeit a little differently from the way you would do it. And the customers are happy and settled; I don't want them to have to get used to a new contact person here when it's not necessary.' But compromise with them if you can: 'If you feel you're ready to handle larger accounts, though, we can talk about finding a suitable large account for you to take responsibility for.'

The rule bender

Rule benders often get excellent results by playing the system or ignoring a few minor regulations – that's why they do it: because it works. These people are a problem for two reasons. One is that the team – or even the company – can be in trouble if their rule-bending is uncovered; the other is that the rest of the team resent their getting away with it. Such people can be approached in a number of ways:

- before you tackle the rule bender, make sure they don't have a valid point. They may be breaking a rule of the team's own making that is better broken – so always make sure the best solution isn't to abolish the rule;
- assuming this isn't the case, stand up to them, for the sake of their colleagues. Resist their argument that their results improve when they bend the rules;
- if they agree to play by the book, give them at least as much recognition and reward for good results, even if the results aren't quite as good as they were when the rules were being bent. This should reduce their need to get results at all costs;
- bring up the matter at team meetings. Don't accuse the rule bender personally; just

raise the issue of rules in general, or the particular one in question. If they see that their colleagues are opposed to their behaviour they may think twice;

- obviously if you cannot stop this person from twisting the rules you may have to warn them that you will report them next time, or take disciplinary action.

The buck-passer

These people are full of excuses for not having done things: 'Robin was away so I couldn't get at the research material', 'the computer went down on Tuesday', 'Pat needed me to produce a report really urgently at the end of last week'. You're just waiting for them to say 'the dog ate my homework'. These excuses often implicate other team members which can lead to conflict within the team. Suggested approaches are:

- be very specific about the targets for tasks you give them to do. For example, 'I'd like this report to be fairly in-depth, say around 10,000 words, and I need it completed, printed and bound by 4.30 this Friday.' You may find that you need to put all instructions in writing for some buck-passers;
- if they give you any excuses just use the stuck record technique. If they tell you they couldn't get at the research material say: 'I can see that makes it harder. But I still need it on Friday';
- occasionally they may have a genuine problem in getting the work done, but don't help them unless it's really necessary, otherwise they'll never learn to sort out their own problems, they'll always dump them on you. If they try to do this, stop them by responding to their excuse: 'I can see it's a problem for you not having access to the material you want; how are you going to solve it so you can still deliver on Friday?';
- if they try to blame someone else don't get sidetracked. If they tell you Robin shouldn't have taken the key to the filing cabinet home just say: 'That's a separate issue. At the moment we're talking about how you're going to deliver this report by Friday';
- make it clear that taking responsibility for something means that you are responsible no matter who actually does the work, and whether or not you're there at the time.

SUMMARY

As I said in the Introduction, just remember that you can't change people's personality. Once you accept that, you stop expecting miracles and you find you're satisfied with a reasonable improvement. But changing people's behaviour can be more effective than you might imagine. To illustrate that point here's a synopsis, with apologies to Max Beerbohm for my inferior prose, of his short story *The Happy Hypocrite*.

The Happy Hypocrite

A dissolute Regency rake, given to outrageous drunkenness and gambling, falls in love with a sweet, innocent country girl. He proposes marriage to her but she tells him that, flattered though she is by his offer, she cannot accept it. She explains that she could only marry a good and saintly man, and that such character would be bound to show in his countenance. The rake's face however is pitted and scarred after years of debauched living.

He is shattered at being rejected by her; and then he has an idea. There is a mask maker in London reputed to be so skilled that his masks cannot be distinguished from a real face. He visits this craftsman and has a beautiful, saintly mask made for himself. It fits him perfectly and no one can recognise him. He changes his lifestyle completely, giving up drink and returning his gambling winnings to the losers he impoverished. He woos the girl he loves under his new identity and she falls in love with him; he moves to the country and they settle into a happy, simple, rural life.

But one person knows his secret. His ex-lover – whom he abandoned when he met the girl he is now married to – saw him go into the mask maker's shop, and recognised him by his clothes when he came out of the shop wearing the new mask. She goes to visit him in the country, and reveals what she knows in front of his wife, who is shocked to hear his secret. The ex-lover asks him to take off the mask but he refuses, not wanting his wife to see his ghastly face underneath. An argument ensues and the ex-lover finally throws herself at him and pulls off the mask herself. They are stunned to find that the once worn and pitted face underneath has grown to fit the mask perfectly, and is now the food and noble countenance of a saintly man.

CHAPTER FIVE

Working together

The last two chapters looked at how individuals can harm the unity of the team if you don't take action to prevent the damage. But many problems that threaten the team arise between two or more members of it. This chapter addresses the following areas:

- **how to deal with conflict between two members of the team**
- **what to do if your team breaks up into factions**
- **how to contain gossip**
- **team stress.**

Conflict in the team

You are in a position to prevent a good deal of conflict from ever arising in your team. If you have taken the action we have already covered in this book, you will have eliminated the possibility of conflict in many areas where it can arise in less well-led teams than your own. You will reduce the chance of conflict between team members if you:

- make sure that everyone is in a functional role and a team role that suits them (see Chapter 1);
- make sure that everyone is well motivated, as an individual and as a team player (Chapter 2);
- ensure that all your team members are clear about their objectives, both personal and collective (Chapter 2);

- do everything you can to minimise internal conflict within people who are stressed or suffering personal problems (Chapter 3);
- create a culture in which people feel able to come and talk to you when they are having problems (Chapter 3);
- ease personality problems in the team by reducing the destructive effects of difficult people (Chapter 4).

Once you've done all this, you deserve never to have to deal with conflict between team members. But we all know real life's not like that.

Training your team in teamwork skills

There are certain skills that we've covered already that your team members will need to acquire. In effect you have to train them to work as a team; like any other aspect of their work there are skills they will need to learn so that they can prevent conflict. Conflict between team members most commonly happens when:

1. **One person or group feels they are doing an unfair share of the work**: either because they are (or believe they are) doing more than they should have to, or because they have been allocated tasks that are less inspiring, important or valuable than others' tasks.
2. **One person or group feels excluded from the team**: because (they feel) they are not listened to, not kept informed or not consulted on team decisions.
3. **There is a straightforward personality clash between team members**.

Different teamwork skills are needed to prevent each of these problems arising, so let's go through them in turn and outline the key lessons in each case.

Unfair workload

The key lessons are:

- everyone should accept that the object of the exercise is to complete the tasks and projects effectively. Tasks are only allocated in order to exploit everyone's strengths and maximise the team's performance. So if for any reason the most effective way to get the job done sometimes involves helping out on a task allocated to someone else, everyone (including you, of course) should be willing to do that;

- everyone should co-operate in seeing that tasks are allocated fairly, in terms of both the amount of work and the interest team members have in doing it. Often one person will hate a job that another one enjoys, and sometimes a task will come up that everyone hates; of course it still has to be done, but the team should make sure it isn't always the same person who gets lumbered with it. It's important not only that no one is unfairly loaded with work, but also that no one *feels* they are. This will still lead to conflict, regardless of whether it's really the case or not.

Feeling of exclusion

The key lessons are:

- everyone should feel able to express a view about any aspect of the team's work, not only the area they work in. All team members should encourage each other in this;
- all information which could be relevant to the team and its work should be shared with everyone – no one should keep information to themselves;
- during team meetings and discussions, people should be encouraged to say if they are unclear about anything;
- there should be a team rule that no idea is sacred – anyone is entitled to question or to suggest alternatives. This should go hand in hand with a second team rule – when discussing ideas, anything goes. All ideas should be welcomed, and treated with respect so people always feel comfortable about expressing their views;
- every time someone makes a suggestion, the rest of the group should hear them out before they start to disagree.

Personality clash

The key lessons are:

- everyone in the team should be trained in feedback techniques (see Chapter 4). They should be encouraged to talk to each other directly – following feedback guidelines – when problems arise, rather than allowing bad feeling to fester. It's important that they accept it as part of their job to minimise conflict between themselves and their colleagues in this way;
- everyone needs to understand the value of compromise, and to focus on the best way

to achieve the team's objectives. They should recognise that meeting objectives and targets is the touchstone against which they measure everything: the method of getting there is secondary. They may need to compromise on the method in order to achieve the end result successfully;

- team members should consciously make an effort to recognise each other's feelings – such as lack of confidence, inexperience or stress – and support each other.

We have now shown how to prevent the vast majority of potential conflicts between team members. On the few remaining occasions – where prevention has failed – you will have to take steps to cure the problem:

- first of all, make sure that all the guidelines listed above are genuinely being followed; if not, remind the team of them and make sure they are reincorporated into the team's working practice;
- call the team together as a group and reclarify the team's current objectives. Make sure that everyone is clear, and in agreement, and make sure they remain clearly focused on these goals.

If neither of these steps removes the problem completely, you will have to address the two people involved face on by sitting down with them and talking through the problem. You have to get them together, otherwise they will each wonder what you said to the other, and they may even misrepresent you to each other. This could make the problem worse rather than better, and it could even turn into a three-way conflict that you have become entangled in. The following guidelines should be followed:

- create a relaxed, informal setting to discuss the problem, at a time when no one is under time pressure;
- make it clear from the start that your job is to focus on objectives and to ensure that the team works towards them as effectively as possible. Their conflict is inhibiting that process, and you want to resolve it for the sake of the team. Explain that you do not wish to allocate blame, you simply want to resolve the problem;
- ask them to accept you as a mediator. Tell them that you believe that talking through the problem will resolve it, but get their agreement that if there are any points they cannot resolve they will accept your decision on them. These can always be reviewed later if the difficulties persist;
- remind them of the techniques of feedback which you have, by now, trained them in.

Tell them that you would like them to use the feedback format to discuss their conflict. Remind them that feedback rules state that they should each allow the other to finish what they are saying, focus on the problem and not each other's personality, and talk about their own feelings and reactions rather than focus on the other person's actions;

- keep out of the discussion as much as possible, except to remind them of the rules if they start to stray from them;
- make absolutely sure that you give no indication whatever of any personal bias. If you think one of them is being more unreasonable or difficult than the other, don't let either of them see it. You are a referee only, so don't express an opinion;
- don't allow them to finish the meeting without an agreement – a verbal contract – about their future behaviour. If one person is in any way coerced into this arrangement they are unlikely to follow it, so you need to make sure that it is a genuinely mutual agreement. Make sure that one of them isn't making all the concessions in order to keep things sweet, but that they are both taking steps to meet each other half way;
- do anything you can to help in your capacity as team leader. For example, they may ask you to reallocate certain tasks, or reprioritise them, or to rearrange the office layout so the two work physically closer together or further apart. You brought these two people together to resolve their differences, so it's important that you are seen to co-operate when it comes to taking practical steps to achieve that resolution;
- arrange a date to review things after a few days or weeks (whichever seems appropriate). This way no one feels they have to commit themselves to an arrangement they might not be happy with when they try it, and if it only partly solves the problem they have a chance later to discuss further action;
- at the end of the meeting, thank both of them for co-operating in trying to resolve the problem. At the review session, thank them for any success they have had in making their solution work. Tell them you recognise that it isn't always easy, and that by managing to improve matters they have benefited the team as a whole.

Factions within the team

If you've followed all the guidelines so far it's extremely unlikely your team will separate into factions. In the unlikely event that it does, however, you need to identify what kind of split it is. There are three factors that can cause a split in the team:

1. **A disagreement over policy issues**
2. **A status battle between two senior team members**
3. **Rivalry between groups in the team.**

Each one of these has a different choice of solutions, so we'll look at them in turn and outline the key lessons in each case.

The policy issue split

There may be such strong disagreement in the team about the collective goal that it splits the group. For example, the team can't agree whether it should concentrate on the domestic or industrial market. The key lessons are:

- you need to identify the problem as early as you can. In many cases this is just a matter of not ignoring it in the hope it will go away. The sooner you take action the better, and if you can pre-empt a split completely that's even better. You can't act too soon;
- call a team meeting and discuss the issues. The aim of the meeting is to reclarify the team's objectives. If you have built a strong team, its members will want to reach agreement and they will understand the importance of doing so. Your job is to make sure it happens;
- once a decision has been made, you need to make it evident that it is final. There's no point in your team members continuing to discuss the merits and demerits of the various options because it's too late. So whatever you do, don't let them think it's open for review later;
- it can help to follow up this session with an increased workload (within reason) or a major challenge to the team. You can often create this by bringing forward a project the team would normally have started work on in a few weeks' time. The object of the exercise is to unite the team in a common cause, and put them under just enough pressure that they don't have time to dwell on past decisions and emotions but focus on future plans;
- one of the best ways to unite the team is to focus them on threats, dangers, rivals or enemies outside the team. If you can make them feel that survival is at stake and the enemy is beating at the gates, internal disputes seem less important. It is on the same

principle (if a little more dramatic) that dictators often start foreign wars to forestall revolution at home.

The status battle split

This can be a little tougher to deal with. What happens is that the factions form around two key players on the team who have different aims for the team, different styles of working, or different ambitions for themselves. The key lessons are:

- this situation can only arise if the two people involved are pulling in different directions in some way. You need to refocus them on the team: its needs and its objectives;
- call the two people together and mediate while they discuss their differences together, following the guidelines we have just covered;
- the greatest danger in these situations will come if you are weak in the way you handle it. You will need to be firm with these two, and tell them that the split in the team could not be happening unless they are allowing it to. Point out that the team is suffering as a result of the split, and that if they are committed to the team they must smooth out their differences and work to reunite the team;
- the most important question to ask these people is 'What is the best way for the team to accomplish the task?' Once you retreat to 'What is the best way to keep A happy, or stop B sulking?' you are on a very slippery slope because people will realise that success depends on the force of their personalities not the force of their arguments;
- if this has reached a critical point, or the people involved are not willing to co-operate, it may well be necessary to point out that if they do not have the necessary commitment to the team there is no place for them as a member of it.

The group rivalry split

This most commonly happens when there are already two groups within the team, say, national sales and international sales, or when the team is made up of two smaller teams that have been merged. In this case a natural rivalry springs up between the two teams just as, when I was at school, there was rivalry between the A stream and the B stream (despite the fact that we were streamed quite randomly, not according to ability). The key lessons are:

- don't assume that this is necessarily a bad thing. Sometimes it encourages healthy competition. If you have, for example, two regional sales forces competing, you need to make sure that the atmosphere remains friendly, that one team doesn't become demoralised by always being seen as the 'losers', and that the rewards are designed to motivate but are not valuable enough to create serious jealousies;
- sometimes you can handle this a little differently and split the existing factions into smaller groups so that each competes with its previous 'allies' as well as with its previous 'opponents';
- if the atmosphere has become tense and some of the rivalry is being taken too seriously, swap round some of the key people – have a reshuffle – so that they can't compete;
- groups tend to have collective personalities. Other teams in the organisation will be perceived as 'clever' or 'spoilt' or 'aggressive'. When two teams merge, each sees the members of the other team in this light. Encourage them to see each other as individuals and this feeling often dissipates. Try sitting members of each team at desks next to each other, organise team social events, hold regular team meetings and generally speed up the 'getting to know each other' stage. Hold contests at team social events in which the teams are mixed up so that rivals become allies.

Containing gossip

Gossip can easily damage the whole team. By its nature it tends to get embellished for effect and often people start to believe things which undermine their confidence or their feelings of security, and they become demotivated. There are two ways to address the problem, which you will need to practise in tandem: prevention and cure.

The best way to stop your team from gossiping about work is to tell them everything they want to know before they have a chance to make it up. As we saw in Chapter 2, if you give your team all the information you can they will be more motivated. They will also have nothing to gossip about. And when it comes to rumours about which they have heard nothing from you, they will be sceptical; after all, if it were true you would have told them about it by now – you always do. Don't draw the line at confidential information either; if you trust your team with this you will motivate them and build their trust in you. Again, we dealt with this in Chapter 2.

Occasionally you may encounter a problem when the rumours are about the whole organisation rather than affecting only your team, and they are true – at least in part –

but highly confidential so you can't tell the team. In this case you will have to go to your own boss and say 'We can't keep this under wraps any longer, we'll have to get everyone together and tell them something, even if we don't tell them everything.' It's a mistake in these cases to use your own initiative, and the best solution is to persuade senior management that it will do more harm than good if they try to keep the facts secret any longer.

Of course, the occasional false rumour will slip past the system. When this happens, you need to call in the person you believe is initiating or spreading it. If you're not sure, take a guess – it won't matter that much. (Remember we're only concerned about work-related rumours. If your team wants to whisper about the fact that John on reception's marriage is breaking up, that's none of your business.)

- don't be tough on them – treat them as though this could be useful information rather than mere rumour. After all, until you've discussed it with them you don't know – maybe it is true. Say to them 'I understand that you've been passing on the news that the sales department may be relocating to the Midlands. What can you tell me about it?' Ask them to give you the details, where they heard it from, the evidence behind the information and so on;
- while they are in your office with you telephone the relevant people to confirm the story. Call the sales manager, for example, and ask whether the team is moving. If the person with you did not initiate the rumour themselves, don't give them a hard time – they'll be feeling embarrassed enough as it is. And by the time you've finished talking to them you may well have rooted out the real culprit;
- once your team discovers that this is how you react to gossip they will think again before they spread rumours in future; no one wants to go through that kind of embarrassment;
- make sure your team understands that if they hear gossip that affects their work they can come straight to you and simply ask you if it's true. When they discover that you're always happy to talk through this sort of thing with them, and that you'll tell them anything you can, they won't need to spread gossip in future.

Team stress

It's damaging enough when one person in the team is stressed, as we've already seen, but if this spreads to the whole team the effects can be catastrophic. Sometimes the stress doesn't come from another person but from a situation. Maybe the team can see it isn't going to meet its targets, or it has just lost a major contract, or been moved to a new building which is depressing and cold by comparison with the last one. Whatever the reason, you first need to recognise that you have a stressed team on your hands, and then control and eventually eliminate the problem.

Identifying team stress

In order to recognise this kind of problem, you need to know the symptoms of it. It's possible that you will recognise these in yourself as well as in others. After all, you can 'catch' team stress along with the rest of them. The following symptoms, if observed in most or all of the team members, suggest an outbreak of team stress:

- lax timekeeping
- low standards of work
- long coffee and lunch breaks
- people talk about 'I' not 'we'
- factions, gossip, backbiting, cliques
- referring to the organisation as 'they' not 'we'
- sulking, snapping or lack of communication
- targets and deadlines not met
- illness and absenteeism
- poor or even hostile atmosphere
- low trust and co-operation
- papers always open at 'situations vacant' page.

Controlling team stress

The first thing to do, obviously, is to tackle the cause of the stress. If it is caused by one person dragging the team down, talk to them and help them (following the guidelines in Chapter 3). If there is a difficult or crisis situation behind the problem, deal with this (see Chapter 7). But you'll have to take other steps as well once the damage has struck, in order to return the team to its usual relaxed, positive state:

1 One of the most common causes of team stress is lack of direction. The team simply drifts because no one is very clear where they are supposed to be going. You need to remedy this:

- call a team meeting to clarify the team's goals;
- as a team, draw up a mission statement for the team to outline its purpose.

2 There is bound to be a degree of stress if the team is over or understaffed. They will feel overstretched and exploited if there are too few team members to sustain the workload, or they will feel redundant if there is too much duplication and overlap between jobs. Call in each member of the team and discuss and agree with them where their own job fits into the team. As the team changes size and shape, these boundaries can become confused and may need reclarifying. Going through this process will help you to:

- identify which team members are bored, overworked or unmotivated;
- find out if systems or processes within the team are ineffective or frustrating to work with.

3 If the problem does not entirely resolve itself after you've taken these actions, speak to the whole team and tell them that you are concerned that they still appear to be stressed and you need to eliminate the problem. Ask them for their suggestions:

- do they feel the team lacks certain skills or has a surfeit of others?
- are there areas where the team lacks experience?
- do they feel that any or all of them need training in certain areas?
- have they got any ideas for changing work systems to improve the team's effectiveness?

4 Find a challenge for the whole team that will not add to the pressure they are under, but will necessitate them pulling together. Look for something that they are quite capable of achieving, but is stimulating enough and has high enough rewards or recognition at the end of it that they are motivated to throw themselves behind it. Something along the lines of a new product launch or a fun PR event, for instance, or planning the redecoration of their own workspace.

SUMMARY

You should find that these kind of problems almost never arise if you've been following all the other techniques for building a great team. But if they do, there are three points to remember which will reduce any problems caused by working together:

1. Clarify the team's objectives.
2. Motivate your team to give these objectives top priority.
3. Keep the team focused on its objectives.

CHAPTER SIX

Interviews and team meetings

Interviewing is a central management skill, and one that deserves a whole book to itself; indeed it has several hundred. We do not have the room here to cover the subject in its entirety. However we are concerned with team building, and every kind of interview involves certain skills and techniques that are especially important for helping to build the team and weld it together.

We have already discussed the techniques needed for the counselling interview in Chapter 3. This chapter looks at each of the other major types of interview and focuses on a team dimension:

- **selection interview**
- **appraisal interview**
- **discipline interview**
- **bad news interview**
- **leaving interview.**

For a group of people to be a team, interaction between its members is crucial. This includes informal communication, but also more formalised interaction between yourself and your team, which is the subject of this chapter. It's all too easy to go for months talking to people every day about operational matters without ever once talking to individuals or the team about how they're doing, where they're going, what's worrying them or what they think they ought to be doing. Occasions for this have to be

scheduled and structured. As well as formal, one-to-one sessions (interviews) much of teamwork centres around group sessions (team meetings). The second part of this chapter focuses on these, and highlights the key skills that make team meetings a vital force in building a great team. It concentrates on:

- **the ground-rules for running effective team meetings**
- **how to run team briefing sessions.**

Interviews

All interviews set the scene for your team's relationship with you, with the organisation and, to a great extent, with each other. For example, if you always hold interviews in a stiff, formal setting, across a desk, say, and allow no introductory chat or niceties, you will be sending a clear signal to your team members that getting on with the job is more important than getting on with each other. We have already seen that this isn't so in a successful team – it gets on with the job effectively because its members work so well together.

You would also be setting up a classic boss/worker scenario, which carries all sorts of traditional implications which you don't want to apply to your team: it suggests that people should do as you say, not disagree with you, know their place, and treat their own subordinates as you treat them.

A healthy team needs a relaxed atmosphere in which all its members are free to express their own views and have their own share of responsibility. In order to foster this attitude, the way you choose to run the more formal aspects of team relationships is vital. Make sure that all interviews follow the same basic guidelines to create a relaxed, if formalised, setting:

- sit in easy chairs, preferably at about 90 degrees to each other;
- have a coffee table between you, not the barrier of a desk;
- offer the person a cup of coffee or tea. One of the great benefits of this is that it's an informal way of saying 'I'm not going to rush you; I've set aside a few minutes to talk to you.' It also turns a boss-employee relationship into a host-guest encounter;

- make sure there are no interruptions; it shows you take the other person seriously and consider them important. If you arrange it in front of them, as they arrive, you will reinforce this;
- adopt a friendly manner – smile at the interviewee, make eye contact and so on. Even in a discipline interview you will want to give the impression that, even though you may not be happy with a certain aspect of the person's behaviour or performance, you are not suddenly prejudiced against the whole person;
- ask the other person plenty of open questions in order to get them to open up and talk freely (open questions are the ones beginning, for example, 'how' or 'what' and which can't be answered with a straight yes or no).

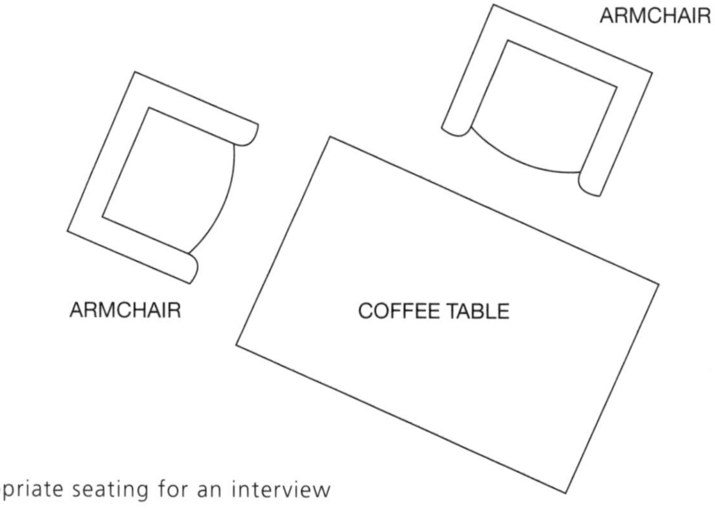

Appropriate seating for an interview

Remember that these guidelines are almost more important in selection interviewing than any other type of interview: one of the people you interview is going to end up as a member of your team, and they will accept the job and turn up on the first day in expectation of a working style and atmosphere they have gleaned from being on the receiving end of the selection process. If you have given an inaccurate picture of the team, you run the risk that when they arrive they won't fit in with everyone else; they may even turn down the job offer. After all, selection is a two-way process – the best outside candidates may have several offers, so there is a sense in which you're selling the job as much as they are selling themselves.

The selection interview

The great strength of successful teams is that they are constructed so that the whole is greater than the sum of its parts. It therefore follows that anyone you add to the team needs to contribute to the whole, to fit comfortably into a team role that the team needs fulfilled, even more than they need to contribute to their own part – the functional role.

Following on from Chapter 1, it is crucial to draw up a team role profile before you start, as well as a job specification and a standard personality profile. Many organisations ask candidates to take a Belbin test or a similar character assessment as part of the selection process. Even if you use a headhunter, it's still advisable to brief them as to the team role you either need to fill or, at least, can accommodate. This has the added advantage that you end up with an assessment of every member of the team, which can prove very useful later on if you're constructing a project team, trying to get to the bottom of a conflict, deciding what kind of person to appoint next time there's a vacancy, and so on.

It is far better to leave the post vacant and readvertise – even if it puts some extra pressure on the team – than to appoint the wrong person if no one fits the bill. If you give the job to someone unsuitable you are being unfair to them, and you are also putting far greater pressure on the team for far longer than if you simply spent a little more time looking around for the right person.

Should you hold a reshuffle?

You may well find that you do not want precisely to replace the person who is leaving. Or if a new post is being created, you might not want to find someone exactly suited to the team's new tasks or workload. A new appointment is a chance to look at the rest of the existing team, before you consider the new appointee. It's an opportunity for a reshuffle. Is anyone getting bored? Are any members of the team ready for new responsibilities? Is anyone overworked? Is someone trying to fulfil a function they're not ideally suited for?

Imagine you're playing magic squares. You have one large square made up of 16 smaller squares in a four by four arrangement. They can't move, obviously, until you remove one – then you have the leeway to slide the others around one at a time, until you have rearranged them into a picture, or number sequence or whatever the aim was. In the same way, most of the time your team is relatively fixed in its structure. But when you take one of the team members, or squares, out of the picture you have a chance to slide the others' roles around, reallocating tasks and responsibilities from the vacant pool left by the departing member, until you have created a better structure. *Then* have a look at the missing square and see what's in it: that's the specification for the new team member. It may be virtually the same as the role that is being vacated, it could be similar but with some new tasks and other tasks reallocated elsewhere, or it might be totally different.

Include the rest of the team

Part of the process of drawing up a profile of your ideal candidate should include a consultation session with your team. Let them know that you will be appointing a new person to the team, and ask them for their comments:

- What skills do they think are needed on the team?
- What personal qualities do they feel are needed?
- Are there any particular tasks they feel the new team member should be able to handle?
- Are there any interests, aptitudes or qualities they think the person should *not* have? (Too many overlaps in the team can lead to frustration and conflict.)
- Do they have any views or ideas on a reshuffle?

Your team need to be consulted not only to elicit their views and opinions, important though these are, but also so that they feel included. If they feel they have played a part in choosing the new team member they are far more likely to accept them when they arrive, and help them fit into the team.

Hold the team meeting, but encourage your team members to speak to you privately as well if they wish. They might see this change as an opportunity to take on or offload tasks in their own job, or a chance for more responsibility. They won't necessarily want to air this idea in public, so make sure they have the chance to air it in private.

If the vacancy is being created by a team member leaving, include this person in the meeting if you can. It gives everyone the message that all the team's members are important to its success for as long as they are there. This keeps departing members' motivation and productivity up, and prevents resentment in the rest of the team if they see you excluding someone who is, at least for now, one of their colleagues. And however you behave, they'll be thinking 'That's how I'll be treated if I leave'.

If the existing team members are going to feel properly included, they will obviously have to meet the shortlisted candidates. In a very small team you could include the other members on the interview panel, but this can be difficult if you have a large team. You could organise a team lunch to which the candidates are invited, or if you are putting them through tests and assessment sessions the rest of the team could attend as participants. However you do it:

- make it a high priority; reorganise the schedule if necessary so that everyone can meet the shortlisted applicants;
- include *everyone* in the team in this meeting; if necessary hold two separate meetings if that's what it takes to arrange for everyone to meet the candidates. Anyone who is excluded is more likely to resent the new appointee, and has less reason to see them succeed: 'It's not my fault they don't fit in. I had nothing to do with their appointment; I never even met them before the day they joined';
- give the team a say. This is not just an internal PR exercise; you should genuinely be influenced by their views. You don't have to select their very top choice (so long as you can justify your final decision to them), but you would be foolish to appoint someone that the team, or a sizeable number of its members, actively recommends against. Since, as we've just established, the team is more important than the individual roles in it, what expertise or skills could the candidate possibly have that are strong enough to outweigh the team's general antipathy towards them?

The interview

There are a couple of points worth making about the interview itself, because they affect how the new person fits into the team if you appoint them:

- dedicate a section of the interview to discussing teamwork with them. What experience have they had of being part of a team (not necessarily at work)? What examples can they give of occasions where success would have been impossible unlesss the group worked as a team? How do they think conflicts and personality clashes should be resolved in a team? and so on;
- notice whether, when they talk about their present job, they use 'I' or 'we' when discussing group or team projects and achievements. Do they refer to their present organisation as 'we' or 'they'? Obviously the word 'we' indicates a good sense of belonging and working as one of a team. (Bear in mind, though, that if they do not

use the word 'we' the lack of co-operative spirit could have more to do with the company culture than their own attitude, or they might say 'they' because you are an outsider. Don't reject a good candidate simply on the grounds that they refer to their present employer as 'they', but their use of 'we' is encouraging.);

- resist the temptation many people feel to focus too closely on qualifications. These indicate a certain level of skill and ability, but lack of qualifications does not necessarily indicate a lack of skill or ability. The reason this matters to the team is that team roles are far more important than qualifications. If you are too centred on degrees and exam results you could reject someone on the grounds that they left school at 16, before you've found out that they have an ideal team role profile to fit into your team, along with plenty of skills which they don't happen to have any formal qualifications to prove. Just remember a few of the successful industrialists of today who have no degree and, in many cases, no higher educational qualifications. To give you a few examples: Sir Terence Conran, Sir Clive Sinclair, Tiny Rowland, Alan Sugar, Michael Grade and John Harvey-Jones.

The appraisal interview

The appraisal interview is the team member's best formal opportunity to express their opinions, ambitions, fears, problems, positive and negative feelings about their job. Which makes it *your* best opportunity to demonstrate your attitude to your team's opinions, ambitions, fears and so on. The impression you give now will remain with your team for the rest of the year until the next appraisal, so it's worth getting it absolutely right.

The general interview guidelines outlined at the start of this chapter are crucial in appraisal; you must arrange an informal and unhurried setting for the interview. If your office doesn't lend itself to this, you'll have to find somewhere else to hold the interview. It's alarming what an effect the barrier of a desk can have in an informal meeting, even when you're deliberately working to counteract it. There are other things you can do as well, to create a relaxed atmosphere and a feeling that you are approachable for the rest of the year as well:

- allow a minute or two to chat at the start – you don't have to fire straight into it. While the coffee's arriving, ask them how their latest project is going, or whether they had a good weekend. It relaxes them, and reassures them that they're not going to be torn off a strip this appraisal. Of course, *you* know that appraisals aren't for tearing people off a strip, but the less confident members of your team will still be nervous even though they know they shouldn't have to be;

- if you and your team member share a sense of humour, allow it to show now and then during the appraisal;
- use 'self-appraisal' occasionally, and mention your own weak points. In other words, when they tell you they've been finding it difficult turning up on the exhibition stand at 7.00 in the morning when the team attends trade shows, tell them 'I was impressed that you arrived on time every day for the last exhibition. I know how hard it is; I'm hopeless in the mornings myself.'

As we've already mentioned, appraisals are not the place for surprises. If someone's behaviour or performance is not up to scratch it should be dealt with at once, and never left until appraisal, even if their next appraisal happens to be next week. This doesn't mean that you shouldn't discuss such lapses, but that the person should know what is going to be discussed. This has two key benefits:

- they will be more relaxed knowing that there won't be anything new sprung on them;
- they will trust you more for not throwing nasty surprises at them.

Responding to your team member's concerns

You will need to use all your feedback skills at appraisal, and ask your team members to tell you their worries, hopes and so on. When they do so, you must respond with more than just a polite smile and the right body language. We saw in the Introduction that the team leader is in many ways the servant of the team, and here's your chance to demonstrate your commitment to your team and its members. If someone raises a matter at appraisal that is important to them, *do something about it*. At worst, you can take the trouble to think about it and discuss it with them again, but you should take seriously any complaint, ambition, resentment or worry that is brought to you. Your team members will, at best, equal your commitment to the team. They will judge your commitment by your attitude in these matters – so aim to find a way to improve matters for the person.

Focus on teamwork

As in the selection interview, you should devote a part of the appraisal interview to discussing teamwork. How does the person feel they fit into the team? Do they feel the team is effective? Could it be improved? What do they feel they contribute to the team? In what ways could the team give them more support? ... and so on. Do make sure, however, that you don't give the impression that you're encouraging them to rubbish their colleagues. Again, the fact that you devote time to this issue signals to your team members that the team is important to you and to their job.

The discipline interview

The most successful teams go for years without any member having to be disciplined. The fact is that if you have selected the right people, provided a motivating environment, listened to them when they had problems, kept them stimulated and made sure they were always clear about their own objectives and the team's, you shouldn't have any disciplinary problems. It's always healthy, when you're considering whether to take disciplinary action, to accept that you must have gone wrong somewhere down the line for this to happen. Try to analyse where you made your mistake before you discuss your team member's mistake with them. The object of this is not to turn you into a guilt-ridden wreck but to recognise that we are all human, and to identify *all* the causes of the problem so as to prevent it recurring.

Is disciplinary action really necessary?

If you've built up a successful team, you need to think twice before you discipline people. If someone who is really motivated and cares about the team does something wrong, it will almost certainly have been a genuine mistake or accident. If they start turning up late for work, for example, it's far more likely to be due to personal or practical problems than down to sheer laziness. If you've got them motivated enough that the job is worth getting out of bed for – well, they'll get out of bed for it.

So most of the time, you're dealing with mistakes and accidents at worst, not laziness or a disruptive attitude. Motivated people who make mistakes feel bad about it. Haven't you been in that position yourself? You realise that you messed up badly and you've let the team down, and you feel dreadful. There's nothing anyone could say to you that could make you feel more guilty than you already do, or more adamant that you'll never make the same mistake again. Your team members probably feel like this when they make mistakes.

If you tick someone off when they already feel guilty, you are denying their commitment to the team. You're effectively saying: 'I'm going to tell you how bad you should feel because you don't have the integrity and commitment to feel it without my help.' Put like that, you can see how demotivating it is. It often makes people feel that there's no point trying if you don't appreciate their commitment anyway. You may have had this reaction yourself in the past: 'I was feeling bad about it before; now I wish I'd messed up even worse.'

If your team members are committed, acknowledge the fact. When they make a mistake, make sure they understand that they have done so, and talk to them about the reasons behind it and the lessons they can learn. But be extremely wary of disciplining them; you may well be doing more harm than good.

The interview

Having said all that, once in a while you might find yourself having to discipline someone. When this happens, there are certain guidelines to follow that will prevent any damage to the team:

1 As soon as you think there might be a problem, tackle it straight away. Don't wait until you're certain there's a disciplinary matter to deal with. There are several good reasons for this:

- if someone is out of line it's likely to affect the rest of the team. They will be frustrated that one person is getting away with something they shouldn't, or they'll be annoyed that they are carrying, or covering up for, one of the team. You need to deal with the problem quickly before these resentments have time to build up;

- it's far easier to tackle someone over a small, minor problem than over a persistent, major one. If they are trying to get away with something they shouldn't, an early and relatively low-key warning could be all it takes to make them see that it's not worth pursuing because they *won't* get away with it. If you leave it until later on, you'll have a much less pleasant and tougher interview to face;

- some disruptive behaviour is habit-forming. Take the example of turning up late to work. Someone may start by finding that you never seem to notice when they oversleep and turn up late. After a while they stop feeling guilty about it and stop trying so hard to be punctual. Still no comment. By now they're in the habit of getting up 20 minutes later than they used to, and when you finally broach the subject with them they find it quite difficult to get up 20 minutes earlier every day. It may even affect how long the drive to work takes, or which train they catch – all in all it becomes much harder for them to correct their behaviour;

- it's not really fair on the person if you don't deal with the problem straight away. If you've let them turn up 20 minutes late for a fortnight they can quite reasonably have concluded that it was OK to do so. Suddenly you tell them it's not.

2 Confidentiality is vital. Never let anyone else in the team know what's going on, and never comment afterwards on any disciplinary action. Your team needs to trust you, and if you talk to them about their colleagues, they will assume that you talk to their colleagues about them. That isn't going to help them feel they can discuss problems with you or admit weaknesses if you ever discipline them.

3 If you are disciplining someone about a problem that has been brought to your attention by another member of the team who is unhappy about it, you must still protect the person's confidence. The team member who complained needs to know only that you have done something about the matter, and that you need to know if the problem recurs. Don't be tempted, even if they ask, to tell them anything about what was said at the disciplinary interview.

4 Be consistent. You will undermine team spirit incredibly fast if you treat people differently for what is essentially the same behaviour. If you let one person turn up late for work for a month before you tackle them, the person you disciplined last year after only a week of being late is going to feel extremely annoyed. And if you let one of them off lightly but give the other one a hard time, albeit six months later, they'll notice and feel they have been unfairly treated. Although you must keep total confidence about discipline interviews, there's no rule that says the interviewee has to. Often when they come out of your office their colleagues will be crowding round saying 'What happened?' So make sure that they all tell the same story, and that you can justify any difference in their treatment.

The bad news interview

No one likes having to impart bad news, but sometimes it's a necessary part of your job. Perhaps one of your team members hasn't got the promotion they applied for, or their proposal to the board of directors has been turned down. As with other interviews, the sensitivity with which you handle this will have a strong impact on the person's view of you, and influence their commitment to the team.

Most of the key rules for conducting a bad news interview have been covered already, but one of the trickiest aspects of this part of your job is coping with the person's emotions. Some people clam up completely, some lose their temper while others burst into tears. All of these reactions can be quite disconcerting if you're not sure how to handle them, so here are a few pointers.

The silent response

You might argue that if someone doesn't want to talk, you shouldn't make them. That's fine if they really don't want to, but people often clam up because they're afraid to show their emotions or because they are – literally – speechless. To some extent you have to judge this for yourself, but it helps to take into account the person's normal character. If they are usually open and chatty, it's a bad sign if they won't speak. If they are generally quiet and relatively unemotional, perhaps they genuinely don't feel there's much to be said. Here are some pointers:

- don't judge the gravity of the news on their behalf. You may think it's a minor setback, but to them it could be a catastrophe. If this is the case, and you say 'Don't worry, it's not the end of the world' they will fear that if they show their feelings you'll think they're overreacting;
- show them that their feelings are important. Make it clear that you've set aside plenty of time for this interview, and that you're concerned about how they cope with the news;
- ask them questions – open questions – to get them talking. And encourage them to ask you questions. Don't say 'Have you got any questions?' because they'll probably say 'No'. Instead say 'What questions would you like to ask?';
- arrange a time to talk again in a day or two, once they've had time to think. This will give them a chance to get over their initial shock or upset, without depriving them of the chance to ask questions or discuss the ramifications of the news;

- as always, don't discuss what has been said in confidence at the interview with anyone else in the organisation.

The emotional response

When dealing with an emotional response the following guidelines are useful:

- some people derive great comfort from a hug, or simply having someone hold their hand, when they're upset. You may find this easier to judge if you think about it in advance. Obviously it shouldn't be a rehearsed action, but a bit of forethought should tell you whether this person is normally tactile or physically distant from their friends and colleagues, and whether the nature of the news is likely to influence their feelings towards you. If the main reason they missed out on the promotion was because you recommended against it, you might be the last person they want anywhere near them. Take into account your respective sexes as well;
- depending on your relationship with the person, and the nature of the news, you might want to have a third person present at the interview to comfort them if they need it. Since the interview is confidential you will have to choose someone appropriate, such as a representative of the personnel department. Or you could start the interview with just the two of you, but if they become emotional offer to call in a colleague they are close to (if they want you to do this, call the colleague on the internal phone for the sake of privacy);
- if they seem embarrassed about crying or showing their emotions in front of you, ask them if they'd like a few minutes on their own. Go and make them a cup of coffee, or make a quick phone call, so they can have five minutes to calm down. Equally, at the end of the interview let them stay put until they are ready to face their colleagues again. For this reason it's a good idea to hold bad news interviews somewhere away from your office and where you won't be disturbed;
- don't give up on the interview. Some people may burst into tears in an attempt – conscious or unconscious – to persuade you to change your mind or do something more to prevent the situation. Most do it simply because they are deeply upset. Either way, you should be sensitive but don't be influenced by tears to change a decision you believe to be right. Quite apart from the need to follow the best course of action, your team would lose respect for you if you were influenced in this way.

The leaving interview

If you care about the individuals in your team – the importance of which we saw in the Introduction, in John Adair's three part model – you want them to be fulfilled. Sometimes they outgrow the team. If the team is successful and staff turnover is low there may be nowhere for them to move up to: the top jobs are all taken by people who don't want to stand aside. Some people develop other interests and want to work in a different industry, or go and live on a Scottish island. It's vital that you support them in this, and are seen to support them. If you abandon their interests when they hand in their notice, you're telling the rest of the team that you only care about them for as long as they are of value to you.

So when someone leaves – assuming it's not under a cloud – treat them in the same way that you treat their colleagues until the day they leave, including (as we saw earlier) involving them in discussions about their replacement. And there's one more way of getting the most out of your departing team member: the leaving, or exit, interview. This is the one member of the team who has nothing to lose by being totally honest with you. The following guidelines should be followed:

- keep the meeting relatively informal; use it to chat a little about their ambitions and find out how much they feel they gained from working as a member of your organisation and your team. Let them know how much they have been valued during their time with you;
- let them know that you genuinely welcome any feedback they can give you – positive or negative. Reassure them that nothing they say will be held against them (or their remaining colleagues);
- ask them for general comments, but if your questions are too broad it can be harder to think of a specific response. So ask specific questions as well, such as 'If you could change one thing about the way this organisation operates, what would it be?' 'What will you miss least about working in this team?' 'Is there anything we could have done to increase your motivation while you were here?' 'What's your general attitude towards management?'
- do something about any suggestions they may have made for change. They may well have told the rest of the team what they said to you – indeed they may even have been encouraged by their colleagues to make certain comments – so the team will know if you disregard the feedback. Furthermore, when they leave they will feel less inclined to pass on their views if they assume from past experience that you will

ignore them anyway. If you're not convinced by any of the recommendations for change that your departing team member makes, discuss them with the rest of the team and see what they think.

Meetings

Like interviewing, running effective meetings is a key management skill which we can't possibly cover here in the detail it deserves. But like interviews, meetings are part of the formalised structure of teamwork, and therefore crucial to building team spirit. There are certain guidelines for running team meetings which all the team should understand, to ensure that the meetings bond the team together rather than drive a wedge between them, and steer the team towards its objectives rather than leaving them to wander aimlessly.

If you go on training courses or read books about time management, they will tell you that one of the biggest wastes of time is the regular weekly or monthly meeting that is held even when there's nothing worth discussing, simply because 'we always have a weekly meeting on a Monday morning'. Scrap this meeting, the time management experts will tell you. And most of the time, they will be absolutely right. But a team meeting is a place where people bond, and develop a sense of belonging to the same group as each other, and you can't over emphasise the value of this feeling.

If your team is small, works closely together and all its members share one large open-plan office, you probably should scrap the regular meeting on the days when there's nothing urgent or important on the agenda. But if your team members work in different buildings, or out on the road, and rarely see each other, the regular meeting may be their only real chance to develop that team spirit. If this is the case, it's better to create an agenda out of non-urgent topics than to scrap the meeting. It's unlikely that your team could have used that half hour more fruitfully than by spending it developing a sense of being part of a committed group sharing the same objectives.

The ground rules

The following ground rules apply to organising and conducting effective meetings:

1 The respect the team shows for its meetings demonstrates the commitment its members have to the team. So it's essential to run meetings on formal principles, however informal the atmosphere. Decisions made by three or four people chatting round the coffee machine just don't carry the weight of decisions made by the same people sitting round a table, without interruptions, and circulating minutes afterwards. Likewise information, if it's given to different people at different times, leads team members to suspect that others have been told more, or have been told something different. So everyone should give priority to attending meetings, they should start on time, and they should have proper agendas, minutes and so on.

2 Involve everyone in regular team meetings and in any meeting to discuss really crucial issues. They won't feel they have a stake in the decisions coming out of the meeting if they weren't present at it and contributing to it.

3 If you hold project meetings, vary the person who chairs them. This kind of fluidity blurs the hierarchy and helps to impress on people that they are not working for the next person up the scale, but for the team and its objectives.

4 Encourage effective meetings in which everyone participates by training your team to follow certain 'rules':

- always ask for clarification if you're unclear about anything; conversely, always be prepared to repeat or explain anything for other members of the team if they ask you to;
- encourage quieter members of the team to offer their views, and keep the more dominant people in check;
- listen to each other and allow every idea to be aired and treated with respect.

5 Make sure that no decision that is important to the team is made without a consensus. This is not the same thing as a unanimous vote in favour, nor a majority vote (where the minority can be strongly against). A consensus decision is one that everyone can live with, even if it's not everyone's first choice. Everyone has to have their say, and it may be necessary to talk through the options and the arguments for longer than you would need to if you just wanted a straight majority decision. But only if *everyone* is prepared to support the decision will they all be fully committed to seeing it through. Often it emerges that it's not the decision itself that people don't like, but the method of implementing it. Thrashing this out often improves the chance of it being acceptable to the team. The team must understand the importance of consensus, and you need to agree in advance which decisions require a consensus. Once they appreciate the need for it they will manage to arrive at it, even if it takes a little longer than otherwise.

Team briefing

One of the most successful approaches to communication within organisations is team briefing, a system pioneered by The Industrial Society. The overall approach involves the whole company, led from the top down, in which all team leaders are briefed and, in turn, brief their own teams. If your team is part of a larger organisation which does not already follow this practice, you would do well to recommend it. However, you can still operate a reduced system with your own team, even without the support of top management.

The principles behind team briefing are:

- people cannot co-operate fully unless they know what's going on (The Industrial Society has found that over half of all industrial disputes are caused by 'misunderstandings and confusion over what management really means when it takes decisions');
- the best way to bond a group of people into a team is to talk to them as a team, about team concerns;
- the fact that the team leader is the one doing the briefing strengthens their position and demonstrates in an effective but non-confrontational way that they are in charge.

In order for team briefing to work effectively, the Industrial Society has identified five rules that you must adhere to. The briefing sessions need to be:

1. Face-to-face
2. In small teams of between four and 15 people
3. Run by the team leader
4. Regular (preferably monthly or thereabouts)
5. Relevant to the team.

Monitoring

If your team is part of a larger briefing system, or if there are teams within your team that have their own briefings, there is a sixth rule: briefings should be monitored. This means that if you brief several senior members of your team who go on to brief their own teams, you need to:

- check any information they are adding to your brief, that is 'local' to their own team;
- sit in on their briefing sessions from time to time (but as an observer *only*);
- make occasional random checks with members of their team to see how effective their briefing has been.

These precautions will ensure that the system remains effective and that no misunderstandings or Chinese whispers work their way into the system.

The briefing

Team briefing sessions should last for about half an hour. The Industrial Society recommends that you have four categories of information on which you brief your team – the four 'Ps':

1. **Progress**. Give the team performance results. Did they meet last month's targets? How do they compare with other teams in the organisation, or with competitors? What new orders have there been? Any special successes or failures? Have the competition brought out any new products?
2. **Policy**. This section covers any changes in systems, new deadlines, holiday arrangements, new legislation affecting the team, training courses, pensions and so on.
3. **People**. New team members, members leaving (including why, and where they're going), new MD or senior management, changes in other departments the team deals with, promotions (including why), overtime, relocation, absenteeism, exhibition stand staffing and so on.
4. **Points for action**. Practical information such as new security measures that must be taken, suggestion schemes, maintenance priorities, correcting rumours, housekeeping details and the like.

A brief is just that – a brief – it's not a discussion. You have set your agenda in advance and you should work through it:

- encourage questions, but not debate. If people want fuller information, explanations or reasons you should try to help but don't get into arguments. If you feel an argument brewing, explain that this is not the time for it but you are happy for team members to raise the issue another time;

- encourage comments and suggestions and note them down, but don't discuss them now. You can arrange an individual or team session for that later if necessary;
- if anyone asks you something you don't know, find it out for them in the next day or two;
- check that team members have understood anything complicated by asking questions to make sure it's clear to them;
- summarise the key points at the end of the briefing;
- find something positive to finish with so that people leave on an upbeat note;
- don't run over time – 30 minutes should be ample;
- give the date of the next briefing so that everyone can mark it in their diary and make sure they are available;
- if anyone is absent from the briefing session, brief them yourself when they return.

Team briefing is one of the most valuable methods there is of building a great team, and as they become used to it your team members will appreciate being kept in the picture about where they're coming from and where they're going.

> The Industrial Society produces a wealth of information on team briefing, based on over 30 years' experience. The material available includes books, videos and an information pack. You can contact The Industrial Society's Sales Unit at: Quadrant Court, 49 Calthorpe Road, Edgbaston, Birmingham B15 1TH. 0121 454 6769

CHAPTER SEVEN

Difficult situations

Some problems can be resolved by getting out your calculator, rescheduling an appointment or agreeing to pay overtime next weekend. But a lot of difficult situations are about people – either the people are the problem or they're part of the solution. In these situations you need to know how to keep the team on your side and get their co-operation.

We looked at situations which cause problems for one member of the team in Chapter 3, and saw how if these aren't contained they can spread to the rest of the team. The situations in this chapter affect the whole team right from the start. Broadly speaking, they can be divided into three categories:

1. **Accidents: such as the building catching fire or the mainframe computer crashing;**
2. **Organisational problems: work-based situations such as mergers, restructuring, redundancies and so on;**
3. **Domestic situations: things like two married members of the team having an affair, one of the team being sacked or a team member dying.**

There are certain rules that apply to every one of these situations, and this chapter looks at these first; it then goes on to examine some of the individual examples in more detail. We shan't be looking at the practical solutions to these problems, but at the team dimension: how to hold the team together and keep it working effectively while the situation is resolved.

The ground rules

There are certain standard procedures that will always minimise the difficulty of the situation, and will often eliminate minor problems altogether. We have dealt with most of them elsewhere in this book in other contexts, but here's a summary of the most important general practices – the seven key rules to ensure you never inadvertently make a drama out of a crisis:

1. Keep everyone in the team informed of what's going on all the time.
2. Assemble the team *en masse* to give them important information or directions.
3. Encourage them to ask questions if they want more information or don't understand anything.
4. Involve them in all key decisions; give them as much control as possible.
5. Be available in case any of them wants to come and discuss the problem with you. That means not only being there physically, but also listening properly to what they have to say.
6. Let them see that you're on their side: putting their case to other departments, senior management or whoever, and finding out what resources they need to cope with the problem and doing your best to provide them.
7. Never lose your sense of humour. Laughter is the best way in the world to reduce stress. And if you join in or even initiate the humour, the rest of the team will see you as being more cool and in control than they otherwise might. It takes the pressure off them because it indicates that you're not about to bawl them out for the slightest mistake.

Accidents

As difficult situations go, these are the real crises. They are emergencies which require fast thinking and fast action. From a team point of view they can be a very good thing, for several reasons:

- they bring everybody together as a kind of Blitz mentality takes hold;
- the team members simply *have* to pull together or the situation gets worse rather than better;

- crises often bring out qualities in people that the rest of the team never knew they had, and the others start to look at them in a different light.

Fire, police, ambulance ... and acts of God

Most managers adopt the same attitude to this kind of problem – they trust themselves to make the right decisions when it comes to thinking on their feet. To some extent this is unavoidable because you simply don't know what the emergency is going to be – the building catching fire, a customer collapsing in reception, a bomb scare, or something you'd never even thought of. Squirrels in the roof eating through the electric cables, perhaps, or a gang of terrorists holding the team hostage. Nevertheless there are certain precautions you can take that will stand you in good stead in most crises of this kind:

1. Make sure your team has at least one qualified first aider. Don't simply ask for volunteers, though. Draw up a list of people in the team who are usually on the premises, and then cross off the names of all the ones whom you suspect would be likely to go to pieces in an emergency. You now have a list of viable first aiders. Decide who would be the best in a crisis and ask them if they would be happy to train. You can't push people into something like this so if they prefer not to, move on to the next person on the list and ask them. If groups within the team are often elsewhere, for example they attend a lot of trade shows with heavy display stands or potentially dangerous demonstration equipment to set up, you may decide that one of them should also take first aid training. After the course, it can be very helpful to ask the new first aider to talk at the team meeting about the main things they got out of the course.

   Take their training seriously. I can tell you from personal experience that if your organisation sends you on a one day first aid course and never mentions the fact again, five years on, if faced with someone who has stopped breathing or is bleeding profusely, you haven't got a clue what you're supposed to do. First aid training has to be topped up regularly.

2. Work out what the broad general categories of emergencies are and talk them through with your team. Plan what you would do if they ever happened. This kind of planning session could be crucial if you ever come up against one of these situations – and you probably will sooner or later – but even the planning helps bring

the team closer together. You haven't got time to discuss every eventuality but discuss, say, what you'd do in the event of a fire and what you'd do if someone collapsed and an ambulance had to be called. There may be other potentially dangerous situations that are peculiar to your business, such as a chemicals leak, or sensitive electronic equipment in the basement being flooded out.

3 Plan in advance which people are the best to fulfil which roles in an emergency – whatever it turns out to be. This is another application of the rule that you can't change people's innate personalities but you can make the most of them. To some extent it will help to discuss this with the rest of the team when you have your emergency planning sessions, but as you'll see from the following list there are some roles no one is likely to volunteer for but you'll want to have them clear in your own mind. When it comes to it, the more aware people are of their primary role (everyone's secondary role is to do anything else that's needed) the more smoothly they will work together, the more valuable they'll feel and the more effectively they'll solve the problem. Roles that should be considered are as follows:

- **the 'yes' person**: it's worth having someone who you keep next to you in emergencies because they take directions well. If you say 'call an ambulance' or 'move those things onto the top shelves first' they do it. Some people will respond with 'Don't you think a doctor would do?' or 'Why don't we move these ones before those ones?' There are times when people can help by coming up with better ideas than your own, but in an emergency the speed of the decision is often more important than its precise nature. If you think on your feet pretty well it's going to be a fine line between which decision is best, and action is better than debate. A reliable yes person at your side will not only get on with carrying out your instructions, but in doing so they will set a good example to the rest of the team. So plan in advance who you will choose for this role when an emergency strikes;
- **the cool headed person**: again, decide in advance who fits the bill. This is the person to put right in the thick of things. They may be good at thinking on their feet, or they may not. It doesn't matter. You can tell them what to do if they're not a great decision maker, you just need them to do the nerve-wracking jobs. They are probably your first aider. If not (you may be lucky enough to have more than one cool headed person on your team) they can assist the first aider, or be the one to check there are no customers left in the building when you evacuate. The team can propose people for this role at the planning session;

- **the decision maker**: often in an emergency there are two places where things are happening. The fire is on the first floor and the people evacuating the building are being checked and counted in the car park. Or someone has to go and stop the flooding while someone else starts to limit the damage. You can't be in two places at once so you need someone to go and be you somewhere else. The decision maker should not only be adept at thinking on their feet, they should also carry authority in the team. This could be because they are older or more senior but it doesn't have to be – they may simply be someone the team has a natural respect for. This is a position well worth discussing at a team planning session so there are no arguments when you say 'Would you three please go and help Robin evacuate the second floor';
- **the panicker**: this is someone to get out of the way as fast as possible. Problem is, you can't tell them that. So find a plausible job that needs doing urgently that gets them out of the way. 'Pat, Robin's not going to be able to fix this leak without some tools. Can you go and see what you can find?' (Not a role to discuss in team planning.);
- **the gregarious one**: this could well be your Resource Investigator. Some crises can only be solved by asking for outside help. Someone needs to call the stores and plead for spare hands to help move the equipment away from the flooding, and beg an emergency plumber to come round within half an hour – failing that they need to see if anyone in any other part of the organisation happens to have plumbing experience. Some people are particularly good at this – they know who to call and they don't mind asking favours. This is another role the team can agree on in advance;
- **the genius for detail**: if someone *knows* that their job is to stand next to you and tell you what you've forgotten to do, they're much more likely to think of things you've missed (this may well be your Completer). You need someone for this role who is going to limit themselves to important things, but it's invaluable having a team member who occasionally reminds you that if there's a power failure that means the electronic gates in the car park won't open for the fire engine, or points out 45 minutes into stemming the flood that it might be wise to cancel this afternoon's appointment with your top client *before* they leave their office to come and see you;

- **the problem solver**: how are you going to get that machine clear of the flood when it's too big to go through the door and up the stairs? Leave it with the problem solver, and an assistant if you can spare one, while you get on with sorting everything else out. This kind of problem can take up too much of your time in an emergency, so give it to someone else. This is another role the team can propose candidates for;
- **the sympathiser**: this could be the perfect job for your Team Worker. It's often vitally important to have someone to calm people down – to reassure customers who are being evacuated because of fire, or hold someone's hand while they're waiting for the ambulance. This is not a job to give to whoever hasn't got anything else special to do. It's a skilled role and some people are far better cut out for it than others. It may even be something that your panicker is good at once their initial shock has worn off.

4 When it comes to dealing with a crisis there are no hard and fast rules because it depends so much on what exactly the emergency is. But things will go far more smoothly if you have prepared, and if you follow, the guidelines above for which roles to allocate to which team members. In general, a strong team that is used to working together will always cope better in a crisis (even a totally unrehearsed and unanticipated one) than a weak or disparate team or group. This is because the members each understand their own role and function and their relationships with each other, and this enables them to circumvent many of the communication barriers that confuse or slow down other groups of people. For example, a good team will instinctively turn to the most appropriate person to take control, regardless of seniority, whereas a disparate group will often fail to 'appoint' a suitable leader. This means that when you assess how your team has coped in an emergency, you will learn a great deal about its quality and strength in the broader context.

5 Some crises are over in an instant and only take one or two clear-headed people to deal with. But some last longer – perhaps you need to ask for volunteers to stay late or work over the weekend cleaning up your flooded basement and rescuing your sensitive electronic equipment. In these cases it's important to involve everyone, or the ones you leave out will feel they're not wanted. So find ways to make everyone feel they helped save the day.

System collapse

The computer has crashed, the switchboard's gone down, the exhibition displays have been stolen the night before the biggest trade show of the year. In many respects you need to handle this in the same way that you handle accidents:

- prepare an outline plan with your team for all the most likely or most catastrophic breakdowns and failures that could happen
- decide which emergency role each team member is best fitted for.

In addition, there are a number of steps you can take to help limit the damage:

1 There is sometimes someone better suited than you to take control in this kind of emergency. Suppose the computer goes down and you know nothing about computers but Kim, your Computer Manager, is a real whizz with them. It's very likely that the problem will be resolved far quicker if Kim is in charge of the operation – deciding whether outside help is needed, and whether it's going to take so long to fix that orders should be processed manually rather than just held until the repairs are made. You will still need to be in charge of the overall picture, but this may involve very little other than seeing that Kim's recommendations are put into practice. Agree in advance with your team whether there are categories of system collapse that one of them should take effective control of.

2 These problems often give you some time to think, and even plan. All right, by normal standards it may not seem like it, but compared to a customer collapsing on the premises with heart failure, this sort of crisis is a luxury. So make the most of it. Resist the temptation to rush blindly into the thick of things as soon as trouble strikes, and hold an emergency planning session with your team instead:

- **define the problem:** the problem is not that the switchboard has gone down, it is that no one can get through on the telephone and you can't make calls out. That means no telephone orders, no complaints, no customer enquiries, no contact with suppliers, no cold calls and so on. It shouldn't take a moment to do this, but it makes a difference if you know that the objective is not to mend the switchboard but to restore communication with customers and suppliers. This may seem like a waste of time, but it's not. If you define the problem clearly like this, it makes it far easier to find alternative solutions. Instead of everyone's mind being fixed on switchboards, they are far more likely to think of temporary solutions such as drafting in mobile phones or visiting key customers by car;

- **prioritise the different parts of the problem**: Which of these matters most? Incoming calls from customers? Contact with suppliers? You may be able to find the resources for a temporary solution to part of the problem. You need to know which part to channel them into. For example, suppose the switchboard has failed in such a way that the switchboard handset works fine for incoming and outgoing calls, but it won't route anything through to the extensions. This effectively leaves one telephone to share between everyone. If you have decided that the top priority is to contact certain key suppliers for emergency orders, and the next priority is for customers to get through, your problem is solved. Use the phone to make your outgoing crucial calls to suppliers first, and then use it only for incoming calls;
- **brainstorm the options**: your exhibition stand has been stolen at the last minute. You could cancel your appearance at the show, you could appear without a stand, you could agree a budget and try to cobble together a stand over the next six hours, you could call your branch 200 miles away and ask them to courier their exhibition stand to you. Everyone should be free to contribute to this brainstorming session (which only needs to take two or three minutes if that's all you've got);
- **take only the decisions you need to**: don't say 'We'll hold all the orders at the moment to put on the computer when it's up and running again; if it's not fixed by midday we'll start processing them manually.' You don't know what will be happening by midday. Maybe you'll know by then that the computer will be working again by half past, maybe only one order will have come in all morning, or maybe 500 will have come in by ten o'clock. Don't make advance decisions – you haven't got time. Concentrate on the decisions that can't wait. Just say 'We'll hold all the orders for the moment' and leave it at that. Then review the situation every so often;
- **allocate tasks**: you've defined the problem, prioritised the most important parts of it to address, established the options and made the decisions that needed to be made now. This has probably taken between three and ten minutes. The next thing is to allocate tasks bearing in mind the suitable roles for each team member that you identified earlier;

- **make sure everyone understands clearly**: you're not the only one who's under pressure, and this is where miscommunication can lead to catastrophe. Stay calm, and invest an extra minute or two in making sure that everyone knows exactly what they should be doing.

PR crisis

This kind of crisis comes in two forms – internal and external PR. The internal crisis happens when your team becomes unpopular, out of favour or in disgrace with the rest of the organisation. Perhaps other teams resent yours for supposed management favouritism, perhaps there have been a lot of customer complaints relating to your team's area of responsibility and the organisation blames you for threatening its reputation. An external PR crisis involves the media or groups and organisations outside the company. Perhaps your team is getting bad press after an industrial accident involving serious breaches of health and safety regulations. Or perhaps your planned new car park is close to the local school and parents are concerned about the effects of the pollution on their children.

All these kinds of problems can reach the point where your team feels pestered or even persecuted. The effects are extremely demoralising and can split the team if differences arise: 'You must have known that the sprocket shafts were faulty when we released that batch.' 'I said all along we should make safety goggles compulsory.' 'Well. I wouldn't want a giant car park right next to *my* child's school.' You can't control the behaviour of the people who are levelling accusations at your team, but you can take action to prevent the team from disintegrating:

- do something about the problem. There are guidelines for handling PR crises on a practical level, which you may already know. If not, there is plenty of literature and advice on the subject. The point is that your team needs to see that you are doing something to dig them out of this hole;
- call the team together – *all* of them, however hard that is to arrange – and talk through the problem. Allow at least half an hour to an hour for this – any less and it will seem that you don't consider it very important;
- state the situation and get them to agree to your assessment. Don't focus on the causes of the problem, simply agree on where you are now: 'The rest of the organisation is criticising us as a team because there has been a high level of complaints

about a certain batch of faulty goods which we were responsible for sending out.' Keep using the words 'us' and 'we' to transmit a feeling of unity;

- keep the discussion focused on the present and the future; don't let the meeting turn into a post-mortem on how this all happened in the first place. Remind them that as a team they all share responsibility for improving the situation and that is the priority at the moment;
- if the general feeling is that the team needs to assess the causes to prevent a recurrence of the problem, agree to discuss it but not now. Tell them that the priority is to look ahead and resolve matters, or grin and bear it if that's the team's preference. Once things have settled, you'll schedule a meeting to discuss how the team can stop the situation arising again;
- now get them to agree on a position, or a course of action. The fact of agreement is far more important than the decision – what you are trying to do is to get the team to speak with one voice and support each other. There may be little or nothing you can do to change things, but you can still get the team to reach consensus (which we examined in Chapter 6), and therefore help hold them together as a team. They may simply agree that the situation is far from ideal but they will present a united front. They may want to agree certain action such as issuing a public apology, or statement, or changing the decision on where to site the car park;
- if they want to make – or change – a decision, remind them that the aim is to achieve the team's objectives, not to avoid unpleasantness. Ask them to be clear about their motives for wanting to change things. They may be right to change, though – perhaps the uproar about the car park has brought factors to their attention which they didn't consider originally and should have done.

Organisational problems

Overstretching the team

We have already addressed this problem to some extent in the team stress section of Chapter 5. However, ideally you should prevent the team ever reaching the point of being significantly stressed. The team can be overstretched because of unreasonable demands from senior management or because of long-term absence of someone in the team – because of illness, a sabbatical or maternity leave, for example. The following guidelines are helpful when dealing with a team that is potentially overstretched:

- recognition (which we looked at in Chapter 2) is vital here. Acknowledge that they are under pressure and give them plenty of thanks and rewards;
- be available. Yes, this is always important but especially so here. It's not just that people are working harder, they are often doing jobs they are unfamiliar with or at speeds they are unused to. So they may well need more understanding, or need to ask a lot of questions, or want help with prioritising;
- be prepared to lower your standards. Again, if people are trying to do more work in the same length of time, something may well have to give. Accept that not everything can always reach the same standard it does when the team is relatively relaxed;
- share the extra workload. If someone is away, say on maternity leave, and you are sharing their tasks between the rest of the team, take some of them on yourself. Or you could free someone else up to do extra by relieving them of one of their regular tasks but not their favourite one, or one that means a lot to them for status reasons or whatever. To be safe, ask them 'I could probably take over some of your work for a while so you're free to look after Angela's customers as well as your own. Is there anything you'd like to pass on to me?';
- do something about the workload where possible. Sometimes the pressure lasts for a predetermined length of time. But sometimes it can go on indefinitely. Eventually your words of sympathy and understanding will begin to sound hollow, and the team will start to feel that as long as you keep telling them they're wonderful, you think that excuses you from ever having to do anything about the problem.

Managing change

This could be caused by mergers and takeovers, restructuring, new legislation that affects the team's working practices, relocation and so on. Some people love change, and revel in the challenge of it. You have to make sure that these team members don't either belittle or leave behind the people who are more resistant to change. The following pointers are helpful when managing change:

- to start with, warn the team of impending changes as far in advance as possible, and fill them in on all the details you can;

- involve them in any decisions you can by holding team meetings and inviting comments, questions and suggestions;
- encourage people to express any negative feelings, and listen sympathetically – they may resist change because it threatens their security, because they know they are slow learners, or because they think it will make their role less important or their job less stimulating. Ask them to be very specific about their objections;
- deal with each objection individually. There will naturally be some genuine disadvantages resulting from the changes; admit to these but explain how they are more than offset by the benefits;
- when the changes are made, make regular checks with the resistors to see how they are adapting. Keep doing this until they tell you they are settled.

The office move

It's worth examining the office move briefly, because it's something that most team leaders find incredibly frustrating. A good team will handle the practical side of the move with little difficulty; the disruptive nature of the process is caused by status issues rather than operational ones:

- some desks or offices are considered more 'important' than others. But the argument never admits this – it's always conducted in operational terms: 'I need to be near the car park to carry in boxes of samples' or 'How can I conduct selection interviews in an open-plan office?';
- it's rarely any use bringing the status subtext out into the open; people always deny it. But if you are aware of it you can often adjust some other status factor upwards: the person's name on the door, their own business card, a change of job title from 'operator' to 'executive' or something else that will placate them;
- take into account that status doesn't float in mid air: it is relative to the people around. So it may be that the only reason John isn't happy with the office you allocated him is because he doesn't think it's as good as the one you allocated Pat, and he sees his role as being equally important as Pat's. In this case, you can use the same approach, but if you also give Pat business cards or a new job title you won't have achieved anything. Try to give these kind of rivals completely different status

symbols from each other so it becomes hard for them to compare themselves with each other. Which is better, a plusher office or a better sounding job title? Hard to say really and, hopefully, John and Pat will find it pretty hard to say too.

Bad news

Bad news can appear in many forms. For example:

- you won't be moving to the smart new offices after all – your team is one of those staying in the grotty old building;
- you've been through the budget and there's just no way you can find the money to take on a temp for three months to help get a key project finished on time; the team members are going to have to carry all the extra workload themselves;
- the board has just announced that it is planning redundancies, which will probably affect your team.

Some bad news affects the whole team and it's not a pleasant task having to break it to them. Their morale is likely to be seriously damaged and it can take a while to rebuild. So you need to be as positive as possible when you tell them the bad news – within reason: unbounded cheerfulness and optimism would be out of place. Here are some guidelines:

- tell them the reasons why the decision has been made. If you didn't make it yourself, find out the reasons from whoever did;
- remind them of the team's objectives and reassure them that these can still be met, which is the top priority. If they *can't* be met because of this decision, agree fresh objectives in the light of the bad news, and reassure the team that they can meet these;
- let them know that you are sorry they missed out, and that you feel they deserved to move into better offices, or to have extra help on the project. However the wider picture didn't allow this to happen;
- sometimes compensation is an option. For example, if they can't move offices perhaps you can arrange to refurbish the present ones. Or if you can't afford a temp for three months perhaps you *can* afford to contract out at least *some* of the work;
- try to give them another challenge to put their energies into, preferably something

you are pretty confident will work out well. For example, if your team has a real talent for organising and giving presentations, try to arrange a key presentation sooner rather than later after bad news, to help distract them.

Failure

Sometimes bad news isn't simply a matter of bad luck. Perhaps the team has lost a contract they've been working for months to win, for the simple reason that their work wasn't as good as their competitor's. Or your team's negligence caused four deaths when a car crashed through a safety barrier that should have stopped it – your team built the crash barrier and never noticed the fault. All the points above apply, along with a few more techniques:

- don't try to cover up failure, admit it: 'We failed.' Make it clear that *you* are not displeased with *them* – because you're one of them; you may all be dissatisfied with yourselves collectively. Let them see that you recognise that as team leader you carry the greatest responsibility;
- your job, in relation to your own superiors, is to take the blame yourself but to give credit to your team and its members (as the old army maxim says: there are no bad soldiers, only bad officers). Your team members need to know that you are with them, and that you aren't putting the blame on them when you talk to people outside the team;
- hold a session to analyse the mistakes or weaknesses. Point out to your team that if you can learn from your mistakes you should be better than anyone next time – you'll be the last people to make *that* mistake again. But it's crucial to identify and accept your failings;
- once the team has done this, remind them that nothing is all bad. There must have been some things that you did well and you need to know what they were so you don't reject them along with the mistakes. This gives you a strong positive note to end the session on;
- once a day or so has gone by, start to joke about it. You might as well, you've got nothing to lose. It keeps the atmosphere light and shows your team that it may not be good to fail, but it's not the end of the world. It will ease the pressure on everyone. There are a few points to bear in mind, however:

- — be wary of joking about a failure that has led to serious illness, injury or death;
- — don't direct jokes against any member of the team (except yourself, if you wish);
- — don't make jokes that reinforce the team's sense of inadequacy. Every joke has a butt, so try to focus yours on things like the competitor that won the contract, the specification for it, any minor mistake that was caused by the whole team and not just one member, minor details that were out of the team's control – anything else but the team and its members.

Internal conflict

Sometimes your team will fall out with other groups in the organisation – management, auditors, and so on. This can unite the team in a common cause, but it doesn't usually help them achieve their objectives in the long run. I have not included industrial action here, simply because it is a huge subject about which several books have been written, and if you are facing this sort of situation you would be well advised to read them. A few paragraphs here won't do justice to a subject that has the potential to destroy companies if it's handled wrongly. I would recommend in the first instance that you contact The Industrial Society, whose address is at the end of Chapter 6.

Working with outsiders

Outside consultants drafted into the team, or auditors, can create a problem. The team may be suspicious, and want to know why – in the case of consultants – they weren't considered good enough to do the job themselves. You need to make sure the relationship with the outsiders is an easy one, and doesn't damage morale:

- tell the team in advance when outsiders are coming in, and why. Explain to the team how the outsiders will help them to meet their objectives;
- people will often not say when they feel ousted, so put their minds at rest without waiting for them to express their worries. Explain that the consultant was brought in because the task was specialised (this may be obvious to the team), because you needed someone objective (perhaps for appearance's sake, so that's no reflection on the objectivity of your team members) or because you couldn't spare any of the team members because their own work was too important;

- treat outsiders in the same way as the team while they're around. If you're taking the team down to the pub for a lunchtime drink, invite them along too. This will help to integrate them with the team.

Theft

Theft is a matter for the police; it's not your job to find the culprit although clearly it is your job to do anything you can to help the police find them. The problems in the team arise when there is a suspicion that it is an inside job – one of your team may be the thief:

- you must carry on as normal. Pass on to the police (in confidence) any information you feel may be useful, and leave it at that. Keep your eyes open, but don't go rummaging in people's desks when they're not there or manically checking up on their petty cash records. They'll realise instantly what you're doing;
- if your team members think for a moment that you don't trust them, it will do virtually irreparable damage to your relationship with them. Then, when the culprit is caught, all the innocent members of your team (which may well be every one of them) will have to work with you knowing that you considered them all capable of theft from their own employer. If you only suspect one or two of them, who turn out not to be guilty, your relationship with them will be even worse;
- set your team an example. Until proven otherwise, your attitude must be 'None of my team would do this. We'll be vigilant but since none of us is guilty we shan't allow it to get in the way of our work.'

Hostility towards senior management

This is normally triggered by some unpopular move or decision; in some ways it's not a bad thing from a team perspective because it tends to create team unity. However, it's destructive in the long run, when you view your team as part of a larger unit. One of the team leader's hardest jobs is to inspire team loyalty to the whole organisation. Joining in the abuse of top management is an easy cop-out. You can't survive as a good team in a lousy company – you need the whole organisation to succeed or you and your team members are all looking for a job. But if the management decision is a bad one, you can't pretend to your team that it's good. So what do you do?

- you agree that it's bad;
- remind your team of the wider considerations that the board or management have to weigh up;
- point out to them the weak points in the decision that they wanted;
- compare your top managment to your competitors', pointing out how much better your managers are.

Domestic situations

Death and serious illness in the team

This is about the most shocking thing that can happen in a team, and needs to be handled very delicately. Your team members will be at their most sensitive and will judge you harshly for any insensitivity you show. Having said that, don't be too nervous, they will see that you're shocked too and they will forgive you any mistakes made through being shell-shocked or inexperienced in dealing with this. Here are some guidelines:

- when you hear the news of death, accident or diagnosis of serious illness, call the whole team together and tell them all at once;
- be prepared for some colleagues to be extremely upset; if you have a company counsellor or doctor, arrange to have them on hand. If the news is unexpected and shocking, give the person's close colleagues the rest of the day off – maybe longer. If you're not sure how long, err on the side of generosity. Never mind what happens about today's important meeting or presentation: if the team think you put work before people they will lose respect and loyalty towards you in a big way. And the strength of the team is more important than whatever is in the diary for today. Just about anybody will understand your cancelling an event or appointment, or shutting up shop for the day, because of a serious accident or death;
- if the person has died, give their fellow team members time off to go to the funeral, and go to it yourself. Make sure the organisation sends flowers, quite apart from anything that members of the team may do jointly or separately;
- give the team plenty of time, maybe several weeks, to get back to normal (depending on the nature of the tragedy). Let them feel they can talk about it – don't allow it to become a taboo subject;

- if you make any mistakes, say so: 'I'm sorry I didn't give you all the day off on Friday. With hindsight I can see that we were all much more shaken than I realised at the time';
- if one of your team members is diagnosed seriously ill but is still working, let them decide how to play it. They may want to keep it quiet or they may wish to tell people themselves, singly or as a team. Or they may want you to tell the team.

HIV

Many people who are diagnosed HIV+ will choose to keep the fact private. But sometimes these things get out, or the person chooses to tell their colleagues. When this happens, the situation can call for careful handling:

- many team members will follow your lead. Make sure you continue to treat HIV+ sufferers in your usual way. Don't avoid touching them, but don't keep touching them to prove a point either. Don't patronise them by giving them special treatment such as setting them lower standards or allowing them to turn up late in the mornings. If they develop AIDS they may ask for certain allowances to be made for their ill health, but until this happens they don't need to be made a special case. The important thing is to let *them* tell you what they do and don't need. Otherwise, carry on as usual and expect your team to do the same;
- if you have certain team members who are unhappy about working closely with someone who is HIV+, call them into your office and talk through their fears with them. Give them literature on the subject or suggest they talk to their doctor for reassurance;
- if the HIV+ team member is happy about it, you could hold an HIV awareness session for the whole team. The person may be prepared to talk to the team themselves, or they may prefer you to arrange for an outside medical expert to present the session. Most fear of HIV and AIDS stems from ignorance, so the single most helpful thing you can do is to replace this ignorance with information;
- once everyone knows the score, has talked through their fears until they are reassured, and has been given all the information they want, make it a disciplinable offence to show prejudice towards the HIV+ team member. If you have fulfilled

these criteria, it's highly unlikely to happen, but you must make it clear that you won't tolerate it. Be sensitive however towards the sufferer – they won't necessarily thank you if they become the cause of everyone else's verbal warnings. In the highly unlikely event that matters get out of hand, talk to this person first about the best way to handle the problem. You may not decide to do exactly what they ask, but you should listen and take their views into account;

- unfortunately, prejudices are almost impossible to get rid of. Your best hope is to keep them hidden, and out of the way of the team's work. Do not attempt to turn prejudiced people into unprejudiced people, simply ask them to *behave* like unprejudiced people while they're at work.

Affairs

One of your team is having a fling with one of the directors of the company. Two married team members are having an affair. What do you do about it?

- the good news is that 95 per cent of the time you do absolutely nothing. It's none of your business;
- it only becomes your business if it interferes with the team and its work. In this instance it's a simple matter of taking the person (or people) on one side and letting them know that you're not happy about the effect this is having on the team. If two team members are involved, talk to them separately, not together, since each one is independently contributing to the problem. They might also feel inhibited and unable to talk freely in front of each other;
- behave as though the affairs weren't happening, in terms of how you treat the people concerned. If the rest of the team think that one of their colleagues suddenly has more clout with you just because they have a special relationship with a member of senior management, you will lose the loyalty of the rest of your team. Let everyone see that it makes no difference and there shouldn't be a problem;
- the other occasional, and certainly uncomfortable, situation you may encounter is when two of your team have a relationship with each other and then split up acrimoniously. Worse still, the rest of the team may even take sides. Again, talk to the two people separately and let them know that they are damaging the team and they must resolve things at least while they are at work. Tell them you hold them at least partly responsible if other members of the team take sides. Then speak to the other members of the

team one at a time, briefly. Tell them 'It's none of our business what is going on privately between Robin and Kim, but I am making it clear to everyone on the team, including them, that it mustn't get in the way of work. If you have an opinion on the subject, I'd like you to forget about it during working hours. I understand that this may not always seem easy, but it's important for the good of the team';

- if the atmosphere is still strained after this, try to keep the two of them physically apart for a while by sending them off on business trips, re-rostering or whatever. They'll probably be grateful. The problem should subside fairly quickly – if they really find it impossible to work together in the long term one of them will probably leave or ask for a transfer anyway.

Disgraced team member

This is unlikely to happen in a well motivated and successful team, but occasionally one of your team members may be disciplined for drunkenness, pilfering or some other offence that the rest of the team knows about. Or they may have been responsible for a serious and negligent mistake that has damaged the team. Here are some guidelines:

- deal with the situation in the appropriate way, by disciplining the team member or giving them a warning;
- then treat them exactly as normal and let it be seen by the rest of the team that you consider that the matter has been dealt with and things are back to normal.

Sacking a team member

In the unlikely event that you have to dismiss a member of the team, there are some basic guidelines worth following:

- talk to the rest of the team members collectively after the person has left. Don't give them any confidential information about their ex-colleague's misbehaviour but tell them that you regret that it had to happen and there was nothing personal in your decision. Explain that you dismissed the person because their presence in the team was preventing the team from achieving its full potential – the rest of the team were probably well aware of this and will understand. If it's appropriate, point out that the person was not a failure in themselves, they were merely unsuitable for the team;

- let them know that you are confident that you were acting in the best interests of the team as a whole, and you are sure that they will now be even more successful. You feel that all the remaining members are valuable to the team and each has an important contribution to make.

It's not always pleasant or easy to deal with these difficult situations, but remember that it's often just as bad for the rest of the team, and sometimes even worse for them. So always treat them with respect even when you're under immense pressure, acknowledge their difficulties and give them credit afterwards for handling the situation so well. When things ease off and you have the chance to breathe again, you will find that if you've handled the problem effectively your team will be even closer and stronger than it was before.

CHAPTER EIGHT

Where do we go from here?

So you've done it – you've built a great team. Congratulations! Um...what happens now? Well, if you sit back and do nothing, you'll start to notice in six months or a year's time that it's not quite such a great team as you thought. That's because teams don't remain static or rather people don't. They get bored, they want new challenges, they are motivated by something different from what motivated them last year or the year before. And the work changes as well: most successful teams generate growth, which in turns leads to more people being taken on to fuel that growth. And teams – especially successful ones – take on new responsibilities.

All these things have the potential to lead to conflict and confusion, or to even greater success, depending on how you guide the team through them. Strong, effective teams can give the impression of being invincible. They are not. Sure, a really good team takes longer to break down than a weak and ineffectual team, just as a strong, mature tree may endure several seasons of bad weather that would have killed a less well rooted and established tree, but any team will break down in the end if it isn't tended and nurtured.

Most of the skills you need to sustain a successful team have already been covered in this book in slightly different contexts. But it's worth bringing them together under one chapter to give you a clear picture of where your priorities should lie once you have built your team. This chapter will examine:

- **training**
- **motivating a successful team**

- **avoiding conflict**
- **promoting the whole team**
- **expanding the team.**

One of the dangers in creating a successful team is that there can be a tendency to think of it only as a single unit, precisely because it is so unified. But it is still made up of individuals with different skills, personalities, motivations, ambitions, likes and dislikes. It is important not to lose sight of the individual, and the need to inspire and develop each team member separately as well as inspiring and developing the team as a whole.

Training

We touched on this in Chapter 2, training is not just a way of teaching new practical skills to the members of your team, such as how to operate the new computer program. It has several other benefits as well:

1. It is an excellent way to teach general skills such as feedback, listening, teamwork (which we covered in Chapter 5) and so on.
2. It makes the trainee feel wanted and valuable. You wouldn't invest such time and, often, expense in training them if they weren't worth it. So training people sends them a message that they are important to you. It also tells them that you think they have the potential to achieve even more than they have already.
3. Training also motivates people because it enables them to perform new skills and therefore take on new tasks, responsibilities or challenges.
4. If you train your team collectively it brings them closer as a group, as they each expose their weaknesses, and identify potential in each other that they hadn't previously recognised. It also creates a shared experience which will, for ever after, give them something in common with each other: 'Do you remember that outward bound training course when we were absailing down the cliff and Jacky's boot fell off?' For these reasons, you should always train team members together if it's appropriate, rather than sending them off one at a time to attend outside courses.

5 Training people as a group also encourages them to apply the lessons when they return to work. They all know what each other learnt, so they will encourage and spur each other on, and remind each other when they forget the lessons.

The training programme

You'll need to draw up training programmes for everyone in the team, and another training programme for the team as a whole. Don't use the classic lazy manager's dodge of seeing what courses are running and then seeing who you could send on them. This is completely pointless, and what's more the trainees know it. Your training programme must be demand-led and not supply-led:

- think through what skills it would be useful for each team member to acquire, both practical and behavioural (such as time management);
- then ask the team member themselves what areas they think they need training in, or would like to develop so as to take on new responsibilities in future.

From this, you should be able to draw up a useful and challenging training programme for each member of your team.

You will also need to think through the collective skills that the team could benefit from learning; these could be anything from project management to customer care, and should include teamwork skills. Put together a programme for the next year so that no one ever goes more than a month or so without some form of training, whether it's a week long residential course or a half hour on-the-job training session.

Variety is important in training, to keep the process fresh, and to encourage the trainees to learn in different ways. In-house courses tend to be more sensible for training in subjects that deal with your organisation's products or services, or its systems. You can always invite outside trainers to run in-house courses. Or you may not need a trainer at all – if you run a sales team for example, inviting one of your organisation's buyers along for a session can be very valuable.

Outside courses are more appropriate for learning universal skills such as time management or for professional updates on new legislation. Residential courses can be extremely good for helping to bring team members together since they will socialise together in the evenings as well. This can be useful if there are several new team members who haven't yet got to know each other well.

And then there is a wealth of ways in which you can train people less formally, such as team crisis planning sessions, on-the-job training, job swapping, one-to-one sessions, videos and interactive training such as CD-ROM. One of the best ways to develop the team as a whole is to hold group sessions (or quality circles) to analyse how the team could do better, sometimes inviting customers (internal or external) to join you.

After the training

You must always hold a review session a couple of weeks after training, to ensure that the team member has understood the lessons and is applying them. If several people, or the whole team, took part in the training you can review the training with the group. If anyone has had special difficulties learning or applying the training, you can talk to them separately as well.

If you don't review the training you won't know whether it has worked, so how will you know whether to use that course again? But more than that, the review session tells your team that it matters that they should implement the new skills or knowledge they have acquired. Otherwise it looks as though you'll never even know, let alone care, whether the training was effective.

The final, and vital point, is that once you have taught someone new skills you must give them the opportunity to use them. If you're not going to be able to do that, don't train them in the first place. Some people are resistant to training because they think it implies that they don't know as much as they should. In fact, your team should see training very positively: 'The organisation thinks I'm worth investing in, and they want to teach me new skills so they can give me new tasks or more responsibility.' It's very easy to put this attitude across to your team, but it will wear off if you don't then give them new tasks or more responsibility. And you'll have wasted your money. Training is a kind of promise to your team that you will increase the value of their contribution – don't break that promise.

Motivating a successful team

For the most part we covered this in Chapter 2. But there are a few points worth making or reiterating when it comes to motivating an established and successful team:

1. People's key motivating factors can change, so don't assume that what motivates them today will motivate them tomorrow. For example, one of your team might give particularly high priority to security. But once they feel safe within the team,

and perhaps they've saved enough of their earnings that they feel they have a safety net, they may find that responsibility and challenge move further up their agenda. Or someone who was always motivated by status may settle and start a family, and start to feel that money and security mean more to them than they did.

2 Once everything is running smoothly there is a risk that some of the team, if not all, will start to feel a little bored and unchallenged. There are several things you can do to stop this happening:

- put new combinations of people together to work on projects. Keep in mind the guidelines on team roles from Chapter 1, but try to devise interesting combinations of people that could stimulate each other into productive and original ways of working. Some people bring out different qualities in their working partners from others, so experiment for the sake of the team and the individuals. Putting people into new partnerships and groups also helps to weld the team spirit together, as team members get to know each other better;
- encourage team members to job swap and train each other in some of their own tasks. This will keep everyone alert and interested, provide useful back-up when people are away, and often brings out strengths and aptitudes that no one had realised were there;
- start to give people a chance to practise leadership skills – after all you need to train up successors, and your team members need to know that they are training to become leaders. Let team members take it in turn to chair certain team meetings (not the monthly team briefing though; that's your job), to take charge of projects or to run team training sessions.

Look for opportunities to give individuals more responsibility to prevent them becoming stale. Even those for whom responsibility is not a key motivating factor are likely to appreciate the recognition and appreciation it implies, and from your point of view the more responsibility people can handle the more valuable they can be to the team.

Avoiding conflict

It's tempting to assume that once you've sorted out all the conflicts and personality clashes in the team, and found a system of working that can accommodate them, that they'll all go away. Once you let yourself believe this, you will probably fail to spot any subsequent problems until they have become serious. For one thing, if you start encouraging people to work with team members they have had little to do with before, some of them won't get on as well as you had anticipated. People who could work together quite happily when there was little contact might seriously rub each other up the wrong way if they have to work closely together for several hours a day.

The other main source of conflict in a strong team is that people can change. In particular, when you give people new roles and responsibilities they may alter their behaviour. The most common cause of this is insecurity – if someone is unsure whether they can handle the new responsibility you have given them, they may respond by becoming strident and dictatorial in their new role. This is because they are terrified that if they show their vulnerability everyone will start to notice that they aren't up to the job. When this happens you need to talk the problem through with them, and reassure them that you are confident they can do the job, but remind them that part of the job is to engender a positive and relaxed atmosphere among those working around them.

Promoting the whole team

We think of promotion as applying specifically to individuals. But it often makes sense to promote the whole team. You wouldn't part-promote a person: 'We're making you a manager when you're in meetings and dealing with people, because you're very good at that, but when you're using the computer you'll still be an operator until you've had a little more practice.' People come as a package and we train them in the areas that need developing and then promote them when we feel they are ready.

A good team is also a package (a unit) and when you've invested so much in building and developing it, it seems crazy to split it up unless you really have to. If your team has reached the point where you feel that the people in it, and the team as a whole, are worthy of promotion, there are several ways to go about it.

If you want to promote the team and its members as a reward for consistent achievement, you don't necessarily need to change its remit. You could:

- upgrade the salary of everyone in the team;
- upgrade the job titles of everyone in the team;
- ugrade the team's 'job title', for example promoting the sales team to the 'Customer Management' team.

This has a far more unifying effect on the team than individual pay rises or job title changes. It removes any cause for jealousy or rivalry between team members, and it makes everyone in the team recognise everyone else's contribution, which strengthens them for the future.

In the long run, it's better to give the team new responsibilities when you promote them. An occasional improvement in title or salary grading will go down well, but the team will be aware that you're not giving them new responsibilities. And you won't be getting the most you can out of them until you give them a greater challenge. So when the opportunity arises, promote them to a higher level in the organisation:

- if they're a project team, make their next project a more important and prestigious one;
- give the team new areas of responsibility, for example, your sales team could take on the responsibility of customer care and start to run customer surveys, help train other departments in customer relations, plan and run exhibition stands and so on;
- if the team grows – through its own successes or because it takes on new responsibilities – it often involves taking on new people. This can give you a chance to promote the team *and* its members individually. If the size of the team grows into double figures it's wise to split it into two or more 'teams within a team'. Now you can promote those people you were training in leadership skills to lead their own small team.

Expanding the team

We have already looked at the problems of merging two teams in Chapter 5, and the process of selection in Chapter 6. Here are a couple more points to consider when you expand the team:

1. Focus on the team types we looked at in Chapter 1; you can irreparably damage a good team by bringing in unsuitable types of people, even if they have all the necessary skills and expertise you're looking for. The better you know your team, and the relationships and tensions within it, the more clues you have to help you. You may have discovered, for instance, that Jason and Jacky get on fine in a group situation but there tends to be tension when they work closely as a pair. Maybe the same happens when Peter works with Jason. If Jacky and Peter are both

Completers, say, and Jason is a Resource Investigator, this suggests that you shouldn't take on another Completer to work closely with Jason.

2 Involve the team in any process that entails taking on new people: deciding what kind of person is needed, producing a job specification and character profile, interviewing and selecting (we looked at this in Chapter 6). This should eliminate any problems you might otherwise have met in integrating the new team member or members into the group. The existing team has to welcome them because it helped to put them there.

If your team expands to more than around eight to ten people, you'll need to split it into more than one team – if people work in too large a group their own contribution is a smaller proportion of the whole and they feel less motivated. You could, as I mentioned before, create two or more teams. In this case you will have to decide, depending on their remit, whether they should split completely or whether you want them to be separate parts of the same team:

1 If you want to split them into independent teams – because of the high numbers involved, or the widely differing areas of responsibility, or geographical distance between them – be careful who you put in each team:

- there's a strong case for keeping your original team together and creating a completely new team to operate alongside it;
- if there are still underlying tensions in your team this could be an opportunity to separate people who are not comfortable working together;
- you may have a lot of team members who need the stimulation of a promotion. If you want to achieve this by moving some of them into a different team think carefully about which combinations of people on the team are particularly effective. It may be that Jason and Pat as a combination generate ideas in a way neither can on their own – if this is the case, think twice before you separate them. Equally, consider whether there are overlaps in the team; if you have two good Team Workers you could put one on each team.

2 You may want to keep your original team together despite adding new people to it. But above a certain size it will become harder to generate team spirit. Large numbers of people working together just don't get to know each other as well.

However this option has the advantage of keeping at its nucleus a team you know is strong. So here are a few ways you can make this approach work:

- make sure your two (or more) team groups work near to each other physically. It makes a lot of difference if they can meet over the photocopier or coffee machine, and perhaps arrange a lunchtime drink together. The social side of team bonding is very important;
- organise plenty of team events. Obviously the whole team will attend your monthly team briefings together, but include both team groups in training, staffing exhibition stands, lunchtime drinks to celebrate successes and so on;
- treat the team as one unit when it comes to team rewards and recognition, even if only one of the groups was directly involved in the success. Make sure everyone is aware that the whole team was *indirectly* involved – that without their support and back-up, and the fact they they were taking care of other tasks leaving the group free to get on with this one, the group could not have achieved so much;
- make sure each team group is fully aware of what the others are doing. Any job swapping should cross over between groups;
- if you can do it logistically – and it's often possible – you can have several team groups and make sure every team member is part of more than one group. So for example, Robin is part of the presentation team group along with Pat, Peter and Liz. But that's not a full-time function, and the rest of the time Robin works on the customer information team group – running surveys, analysing complaints and so on – with Kim and Jason. Some people could be part of three or even four team groups. This ensures that no working group is too large, but the mix and match factor means that everyone feels part of a unified team. However, bear in mind:
- it's not a good idea to involve anyone in too many team groups as this can lead to conflicting demands and priorities, but some team groups may only be active occasionally and members may only have to devote, say, a day a month to them;
- your team members will need to be very clear – with your help – about where their priorities lie. What if there's a crisis in both team groups at once? Make sure that everyone has a primary and a secondary (or several secondary) team group(s), so they feel there is somewhere where they have a core role. Equally, make sure that each group contains members for whom that group is a primary one and others

for whom it is secondary. This sounds like a logistical nightmare, but if you talk to anyone who has ever planned a school timetable they'll tell you how easy this is by comparison. With a little thought you can make the system work as smoothly as the best-run school. You may look at the system and see a spider's web of confusion, but each team member looks at it and simply sees two or perhaps three functions that they perform;

- one of the benefits of this approach is that if any team member is uncomfortable in any role, or feels inadequate, or has difficulties getting on with someone in the team group, they don't have to be in that situation all the time. While they are working on the problem, they have the confidence of knowing that they are good at the other part of their job, or the relief of being able to take a break from someone they don't hit it off with – which often helps to keep conflicts at a manageable level;
- another advantage of this approach is that with plenty of team groups, you will have plenty of team group leaders. This gives them challenge, status and responsibility, and the chance to learn leadership skills. Give as many people as you can an opportunity to lead a team group – it helps to develop their skills and it breaks down hierarchical barriers in the team.

Conclusion

This should be enough to convince you, if you needed it, that you can't just sit back and relax once you've built your team. On the contrary, a good team leader can *never* really relax. However, that's no cause for despair; you need a challenge as much as everyone else in your team does, and yours is to make sure the team maintains its high standards. And your reward? Well, the team is reward enough. Perhaps the best way to explain this is to give you an example.

I know a theatre director, Geoff Bullen, who directed a production of John Steinbeck's *Of Mice and Men* which was successful enough to transfer to the West End. It opened to superb reviews which praised the actors' performances, the set design, the lighting and, frequently, his excellent direction. But despite all the accolades for his own particular contribution, the review of which Geoff was proudest was the one which said that the overriding impression of the performance was that it was a team production.

Some acting parts may have been far larger than others, the set design may have been more crucial than the sound quality, but – according to this reviewer – you really didn't notice; you just saw a unified team in which everyone played an important part.

My initial response to Geoff's pride in this review was to admire his magnanimity in being happiest when he could share the credit with the rest of the team. But in fact, as any true team leader will tell you, there is no greater reward than the privilege of being part of a great team and the satisfaction of having played a vital role in building it.

Index